ASTONISHING WOMEN ARTISTS

ASTONISHING WOMEN ARTISTS

by Heather Ball

Second Story Press

Library and Archives Canada Cataloguing in Publication

Ball, Heather, 1978-
Astonishing women artists / by Heather Ball.

(The women's hall of fame series) Includes bibliographical references.
ISBN 978-1-897187-23-4

I. Women artists—Biography—Juvenile literature. I. Title.
II. Series: Women's hall of fame series

N40.34 2007   j709.2'2   C2007-900000-2

Copyright © 2007 by Heather Ball

Edited by Sandra Braun
Designed by Melissa Kaita

Printed and bound in Canada

Second Story Press gratefully acknowledges the support of the Ontario Arts Council and the Canada Council for the Arts for our publishing program. We acknowledge the financial support of the Government of Canada through the Book Publishing Industry Development Program.

ONTARIO ARTS COUNCIL
CONSEIL DES ARTS DE L'ONTARIO

Canada Council   Conseil des Arts
for the Arts   du Canada

Published by
Second Story Press
20 Maud Street, Suite 401
Toronto, ON
M5V 2M5

www.secondstorypress.ca

TABLE OF CONTENTS

For my grandparents,
Bill and Rhoda Hayes

INTRODUCTION

Art, like beauty, is in the eyes of the beholder. If you look at a painting, you might see something that moves you to feel great joy, while the person next to you might see and feel something quite different. Although art is often displayed in public galleries and museums, it is very personal. When artists create something, they are putting their soul into the work, hoping that at least one viewer will recognized that and feel a connection to the piece. Artists have a special way of seeing the world, and every successful artist has a unique vision.

It's hard to believe that less than a hundred years ago, women weren't allowed to attend the best art schools. Their work was not considered as good as that of male artists. They weren't taken seriously as artists, simply because of their gender. With few or no role models, women artists had to forge their own paths.

In this book, you will read about ten women who made art their lives. They all had struggles and challenges to overcome, but they all used their art as way to work through their difficulties. They never gave up. Artemisia Gentileschi overcame a traumatic event to become one of the very few female painters of the seventeenth century. Elisabeth Vigée Le Brun wasn't allowed to take art classes because she was a woman, so she taught herself — and became a successful artist and businesswoman. Emily Carr could barely afford

1

to eat, but she kept up her painting and became one of Canada's most recognized artists. Georgia O'Keeffe went against convention and painted more from her heart than from the examples in art class and Americans embraced her unique way of seeing the world. Louise Nevelson worked at her sculpture for more than thirty years before she got the recognition she deserved. Kenojuak Ashevak had no idea that she wanted to create art, but when she began drawing to express her Inuit culture, she found she couldn't stop. Frida Kahlo had a famous artist husband, but she never let herself be overshadowed. Her deeply personal work carved her a place in history as the soul of Mexico. Elizabeth Catlett was the victim of racism and sexism, but she didn't let ignorance or negative comments stop her from creating the art that was in her soul. Faith Ringgold searched for a way to express herself both as an African American and as a woman, and she found her outlet for expression through her story quilts. Mary Pratt struggled to balance her identity as a wife and mother with her desire to be an artist until she found that she could be all these things.

Today, more and more women are becoming recognized artists. In fact, some of the most famous artists are women. After you've read this book, I hope you go beyond its pages and find out about other women artists. Speak to your teachers, librarians, or art teachers and ask them if they have favorite female artists. Or maybe visit a museum or gallery and discover some for yourself. And if you feel particularly inspired, pick up a pencil or a paintbrush, get your hands in some clay, find some colored thread or construction paper, and see what you can create. In art, the only limit is your imagination.

Artemisia Gentileschi

1593 - 1652

ART SPEAKS FOR ITSELF

Hundreds of years ago, even if a woman had artistic talent, she wasn't always allowed to practice her skills. Or if she *was* able to hone her art, she had few female role models to look up to and had to work hard to prove herself as a serious artist on her own terms. Artemisia Gentileschi, one of the few successful professional female artists in seventeenth-century Europe, was a trailblazer who worked in the male-dominated art world and became a role model herself.

Artemisia was born on July 8, 1593, in Rome, Italy. She was the oldest of four children. Her father, Orazio Gentileschi, was a well-known painter and her mother, Prudentia Montone, raised the family.

No one expected, or even imagined, that Artemisia would grow up to become an artist, least of all her father. In Italy in the late-sixteenth and early-seventeenth centuries, women didn't have many choices in their lives. It was very rare for a woman to have a career. A woman's options were to marry and have children or to become a nun, which is what Orazio wanted his first-born daughter to become.

The Roman art scene was very exciting when Artemisia was growing up. Many new churches and palaces were being built and then adorned with paintings. Artemisia was surrounded by artists — always male — because Orazio had many friends who were also painters. Her own godfather was a painter named Pietro Rinaldi; her brother Giovanni's godfather was the artist Giuseppe Cesari; and her brother Giulio's godfather was Wenzel Coebergher, a Flemish artist. Being surrounded by so much creativity no doubt influenced Artemisia, and she tried painting as soon as she was old enough.

By the time Artemisia was about nine years old, the artist Caravaggio had become very popular. People were familiar with many of his works, such as his painted decorations on the church of San Luigi dei Francesi, because they were in public places in Rome. He painted biblical scenes that rocked the art world because they were so dramatic, realistic, and decorative. This way of painting eventually became known as the baroque style. People also said that Caravaggio used live, nude models for his paintings.

In 2002, the Metropolitan Museum of Art in New York City held a special exhibition entitled, "Orazio and Artemisia Gentileschi: Father and Daughter Painters in Baroque Italy." It featured paintings by Orazio and thirty-five by Artemisia, and was the first exhibition to explore the works of these two artists in depth.

This was not a common practice at the time and was considered shocking. Artemisia probably met Caravaggio several times, because when she was little, he visited the Gentileschi household often to borrow props and supplies from Orazio. Caravaggio left Rome in 1606 when Artemisia was still very young, but his new and exciting painting style and his outgoing personality were often discussed among Italian artists. Many scholars believe Caravaggio was a big influence on Artemisia's work.

Artemisia's father supported his family by doing a lot of work on commission, creating paintings for churches and chapels in Rome. Artemisia no doubt watched him work, wishing she could pick up a brush and bring stories to life just like her father.

In 1605, when Artemisia was only twelve years old, her mother died in childbirth. It was a very difficult time for the whole family, and probably forced Artemisia to grow up quite quickly. As the only daughter, she had to pitch in and help fill her mother's role. The Gentileschis were not rich, so the four children, especially Artemisia, a girl, didn't have a chance to go to school like the children of noble parents. To take the children's minds off of the sadness they felt, Orazio decided to give them painting lessons. He hoped that maybe one of his sons would show artistic talent. To his great surprise, Artemisia was the only one with a natural flair for painting. Orazio was shocked and thrilled, and began focusing his attention on sharpening her artistic skills.

By the time Artemisia was a teenager, her father knew she would become an accomplished artist, and he often bragged about his daughter's talent. He even went so far as to say that in the art world, she had no equal. Artemisia relied on her father for guidance and instruction in her art. As a woman, she wasn't allowed to travel to art school, get scholarships, or work with outside teachers.

Orazio tried hard to give his daughter a solid artistic education. One summer afternoon, he sent her out by carriage with friends and family members to visit three of Rome's main churches: Santa Maria Maggiore, St. Peter's, and the Quirinal Palace. He wanted her to observe the magnificent paintings that decorated the churches, and he wanted her to see the artists at work. This way, Artemisia was exposed to many styles of art, so she could go beyond her father's teachings.

Many of Artemisia's paintings have been lost or destroyed in the centuries since she was alive, so scholars don't have her full body of work to study. Artemisia's first known painting is *Susanna and the Elders*, which she signed and dated 1610, when she was just seventeen. The painting tells the biblical story of Susanna, a young woman who had to defend herself against the unwanted sexual advances of some corrupt men. Using heroic women as subjects became Artemisia's favorite theme. At the time, Artemisia had only been painting for a few years, but those who saw the work were very impressed and agreed that it appeared to have been painted by someone much older.

Artemisia's talent developed quickly, because she devoted a lot of time to practicing painting. In the seventeenth century, people believed that women, particularly young and pretty women like Artemisia, were not supposed to go out alone, not even to the market. So Orazio made his daughter stay home most of the time. Although it was difficult for such a creative spirit to be so confined, Artemisia had no choice but to obey the rules. Artists, models, and students were constantly coming and going from her house, so luckily she was not as alone as she might otherwise have been.

One artist with whom Artemisia had regular contact was Agostino Tassi. He was a painter from Florence who worked with Orazio. Together, they created *Musical Concert Sponsored by Apollo and the Muses*. In the painting is a young woman holding a fan, which many scholars believe is the exact image of Artemisia.

Agostino was a skilled artist, and he had a special talent for perspective (an art technique that gives depth to a picture and makes it look three dimensional). Orazio asked Agostino if he would give Artemisia a few lessons in perspective to make her an even better artist, and Agostino agreed. Orazio couldn't have known it at the time, but it was the worst idea he had ever had.

During a lesson at the Gentileschi house in the spring of 1611, when Orazio was out working, Agostino attacked Artemisia. She fought him back with all of her strength, but he was much bigger than she and he sexually assaulted her. She was traumatized by the horrible event and told her father as soon as he returned. In the Roman culture of the time, such an attack had as much to do with the victim's family as with the victim herself. Not only had Agostino hurt Artemisia terribly, but he had also violated Orazio's trust. Both violations were unforgivable.

Agostino Tassi went to trial for assaulting Artemisia in 1612. The court documents of the eight-month-long trial still exist today, and they show what a horrible experience it was for the young woman. Agostino denied that he had even committed the crime. He called Artemisia a liar and attacked her reputation. He even insulted the character of her mother, who he had never known. Artemisia had to fend off many false accusations, and her character was questioned constantly. In court, it was up to Artemisia to prove that she was telling the truth. In a ghastly courtroom practice, Artemisia, the victim, was tortured. Her fingers were squeezed until she was in a lot of pain. Members of the court thought doing so would force her to confess that she had made up the whole story. But Artemisia was a brave and fiery young woman. She didn't change her story once.

In the end, the court believed Artemisia. When the eight-month trial was over, Agostino was found guilty. He was sentenced to be banished from Rome for five years, but no one ever enforced the punishment. Orazio wanted to get his daughter away from the scandal and the bad memories in Rome. A month after the trial ended, Artemisia married Pietro Antonio di Vincenzo Stiattesi, an artist from Florence. They moved to Florence shortly after.

After the humiliating trial, many expected that Artemisia would stop painting, live a quiet life, and fade into the background. But for such a strong woman, that was out of the question. Artemisia refused to let the awful experience ruin her life and was determined to rise above it. She put the past behind her and started a new life in Florence. In fact, it was around the time of the trial that Artemisia painted one of her best-known works, *Judith Slaying Holofernes*. In this painting, a Jewish maid tries to stop an attack against her people. The painting is a dramatic, violent image, the kind that was fashionable in baroque art at the time. Artemisia would paint many works based on Judith's story in the years to come.

She began working as the protégée (someone who trains in a craft or skill with a more experienced person) of Michelangelo Buonarroti the Younger, a family friend who had great faith in Artemisia's talents. He was the great-nephew of Michelangelo, one of the most famous artists to ever come from Italy. Artemisia was commissioned to help paint decorations on his house to honor his great-uncle in August of 1615. On the walls, he wanted scenes that represented Michelangelo's life, and on the ceiling,

> Artemisia met a lot of famous people in Florence, such as the astronomer-mathematician Galileo. During the Spanish Inquisition, Galileo moved to Florence looking for safety. He and Artemisia had a long friendship and wrote many letters to each other during their lives.

he wanted scenes that showed the artist's funeral. Other male artists worked on the project as well, and scholars believe that Artemisia, most likely the only woman, was paid fairly for her work.

Artemisia was accepted into Florence society quite quickly, both as an artist and as a woman. By 1616, she had become the first woman to ever be accepted as an official member of the Accademia del Disegno, a prestigious arts academy. She was also supported by members of the wealthy Medici family, who helped artists financially so they could work. The Medicis, particularly the Grand Duke Cosimo and Duchess Maria Maddalena, were strong supporters of arts at the time, and to have them as patrons helped Artemisia's career tremendously.

Artemisia's painting *Judith and Her Maidservant*

Artemisia probably saw a lot of court ceremonies and festivals, which often involved elaborate costumes and theatrical shows. She painted many commissions for the Medicis; however, many are now lost. We know about them only through some of Artemisia's letters or other written records that still remain.

Around 1620, Artemisia returned to Rome and moved into a house on the Via del Corso. She had been missing her family and friends, and was having some personal problems. Artemisia's marriage was not going well. She and her husband weren't close, and perhaps he was even jealous of her achievements. Artemisia also got a lot of attention from other men, which bothered Pietro. One night, Pietro awoke to hear a group of men serenading Artemisia from the street, and he was very jealous. To make matters even more difficult, Artemisia had suffered many miscarriages. She gave birth to only one child, a daughter, who survived. She named her Prudentia after her mother. Pietro left a couple of years after Prudentia was born, and Artemisia became a single mother.

When the Grand Duke Cosimo died in 1621, Artemisia no longer had a patron. She worried about having enough money to support Prudentia, so she set about looking for a new patron. She spent some time in Genoa and in Venice and created a painting for King Philip IV of Spain. She also continued to paint using her theme of strong female characters. *Judith and Her Maidservant*, painted around 1625, and *Lucretia* and *Cleopatra* have famously strong women as their subjects. In 1630, Artemisia also completed one of her most notable works, *Self-Portrait as the Allegory of Painting*.

> Because a lot of Artemisia Gentileschi's life is not documented, her story has inspired many works of fiction. At least four novels have been written (*Artemisia, Life without Instruction, The Passion of Painting,* and *The Passion of Artemisia*) and one movie (*Artemisia*) has been made to interpret her life.

For most of the 1630s, Artemisia lived in Naples. Although she didn't like the city very much (she thought it was too expensive), it had a lot of opportunities for her to earn a living through commissions. She did find many patrons there, mostly dukes and duchesses. But she was an ambitious woman and began to search outside of her country for patron opportunities. Around 1638, she moved to England and lived at the court of King Charles I and Queen Henrietta Maria. She also reunited with her father, who had been working in England for ten years. He was about 75 years old and still painting. Father and daughter worked together on Orazio's commission to decorate the ceiling of the Queen's house at Greenwich. In the end, Orazio got most of the credit, although many scholars agree that Artemisia, who was younger and had the energy to do more work, probably did more than her fair share.

> Other female artists also had success in the seventeenth century, though Artemisia was one of the most successful. Examples of her peers include Lavinia Fontana, Sofonisba Anguissola, and Elisabetta Sirani.

Artemisia spent the last ten years of her life in Naples, working steadily. Her patron was Don Ruffino from Sicily. By this time, Artemisia had become a celebrated artist, and collectors and royalty wanted her work. And — as her letters show — Artemisia was a smart businesswoman. She insisted on getting paid a portion of her fees in advance, and she never gave a final price for a work until it was finished. She also refused to send sketches ahead of time, fearing they might be stolen.

In 1653, Artemisia Gentileschi died in Naples. She was sixty years old. Only about thirty-five of Artemisia's paintings and a few dozen letters have survived the centuries since her death. Through these, as well as court documents and documents from patrons, scholars have been able to piece together her life, though much of it still remains mysterious. What we do know is that in her lifetime, Artemisia was not only a respected woman, but also a respected artist, even though the odds were against her. When her life was turned upside down by trauma, she let the world know that she was not going to remain a victim. She made her own path in a man's world and did so on the strength of her great talents. As she once wrote about her art, "The works speak for themselves."

To take a virtual tour through some of Artemisia paintings, visit The Life and Art of Artemisia Gentileschi at **www.artemisia-gentileschi.com**.

ELISABETH LOUISE VIGÉE LE BRUN

1755 - 1842

REVOLUTIONARY ARTIST

Up until the twentieth century, most people thought a woman needed the support of either a man or her family to live, because she couldn't have a career of her own. Elisabeth Vigée Le Brun was a hugely successful painter, who proved these ideas wrong hundreds of years before public opinion would change.

Elisabeth Louise Vigée was born on April 16, 1755, in Paris, France. Her father, Louis, was an artist who painted people's portraits, but he was not very successful. Her mother, Jeanne Maissin, was a hairdresser. They were married for five years before Elisabeth came along.

At that time in France, it was normal for middle-class families to hire a wet nurse (a sort of nanny) to take on the daily responsibilities of raising a baby, in place of the mother. For the first few years of Elisabeth's life, she saw her wet nurse more than she saw her parents.

When Elisabeth was three, the Vigées had another child, a boy named Louis-Jean-Baptiste-Etienne. The family was overjoyed, but young Elisabeth couldn't help feeling jealous. Her mother doted on Louis Jr. and ignored Elisabeth a lot of the time. It was very hurtful because Elisabeth wasn't the most confident child. She was very thin and she thought her arms and legs were growing faster than the rest of her body, which made her feel awkward. But Louis Sr. had a special place in his heart for his daughter. Her father saw something remarkable in her, and told her that she would grow up to leave her mark on the world.

When Elisabeth was six years old, she was enrolled in the Convent of the Trinité. She wasn't there to become a nun, but rather to get a good education that would make her a proper young lady. She learned how to read, write, sew, and embroider, and she learned some mathematics.

Elisabeth's passion wasn't for any of those subjects. Her passion was drawing. She drew and sketched whenever she could — in the margins of her notebooks and on scraps of paper. She was even inspired to draw charcoal pictures on the walls of her dorm room, but when the nuns saw them, they punished her. Louis Sr. knew his daughter was a good child and that she had a particular talent for art. When he saw her pictures, he said, "You will be a painter, my child!"

On May 9, 1767, Elisabeth's father died. She was only twelve at the time and was finished with her classes at the convent. She and Louis Sr. had bonded over their artwork, and now she was without her biggest supporter. Dealing with the loss was extremely difficult for the young girl, particularly when her mother remarried just a few months later. Elisabeth's new stepfather was a jeweler named Jacques Francois Le Sèvre. He had his own store on the rue Saint-Honoré. Elisabeth didn't like him much. She thought he was trying to replace her father. Plus, he was a grumpy man who was known for being stingy with his money.

To keep her mind off her grief, Elisabeth and her best friend, Rosalie Bocquet, took drawing lessons from Monsieur Gabriel Briard. Gabriel was an academic and history painter, but not well known. The girls had to go to his studio, where he would critique their work and offer advice on how to improve it. They weren't allowed to attend his regular classes, because those lessons were for boys only.

Since she was forbidden to attend formal art classes because she was a girl, Elisabeth had to teach herself a lot about painting. She did so by visiting private collections, where she studied works by master European painters such as Rembrandt and Peter Paul Reubens. Although Elisabeth started out by painting some landscapes, she found people the most interesting. In the eighteenth century, it was fashionable for upper-class people to have their portraits painted, much like we have family photographs taken today. To hone her skills as a portraitist, Elisabeth used her mother and her brother as models. One of her earliest works from when she was a teenager in 1773, is a portrait of her brother. He is holding a book and pen, and has an optimistic twinkle in his eye. Even from an early age, Elisabeth had a knack for finding the best in people and capturing it on canvas.

Elisabeth painted her first commissioned portrait (a portrait that someone paid her to create) when she was in her teens. After only a few years of practicing, she was making her own money as a professional painter by the time she was seventeen. However, because she lived at home with her mother and stepfather, she didn't have total control over the money she earned. Her stepfather spent a lot of Elisabeth's money on himself, and she promised herself that when she was old enough, she would be in control of her earnings and her work.

Most recognized painters in Elisabeth's time belonged to influential art groups. Not only did being a member prove that you were a respected artist, but it also gave you a special license to practice your craft. It was against the law to run a studio and paint portraits without a license. But Elisabeth wasn't allowed to join most of these groups, for the simple fact that she was a woman. She especially wanted to join the Académie Royale de Peinture et de Sculpture (Royal Academy of Painting and Sculpture), but the members were all men who didn't want a woman among them.

Elisabeth's attitudes were conservative for her time; she believed in the monarchy (the royal family) even when many citizens of France were becoming displeased and wanted big political changes. However, unlike most people, she believed strongly in her right as a female artist to be treated the same as a male artist. The situation seemed almost impossible. She could not get a license because she was a woman, and she wasn't supposed to practice art without a license.

In 1774, Elisabeth's studio was shut down and her supplies were seized. She immediately applied for membership to the same group to which her father had belonged — the Académie Saint Luc. It was not as well regarded, but she was granted membership and licensed as a master painter that same year. After getting her license, Elisabeth developed even more quickly as a painter and her reputation grew.

In 1775 her stepfather retired and moved the family to an apartment on the rue de Cléry. Their new neighbor was Jean Baptiste Pierre Le Brun. He was an artist (although not a very good one) and an art restorer and critic, but his main job was as an art dealer. He liked Elisabeth right away, and offered to let her study and copy paintings from his collection as practice.

After a few months, Jean asked her to marry him. At first, Elisabeth hesitated. She was only about twenty, and he was seven years older. Elisabeth had many other admirers, but she wasn't interested in romance. She didn't want anything to distract her from painting. Plus, she wasn't convinced that marriage was necessary for her. After all, she made

> Adélaide Labille-Guiard (1749–1803) was another successful female French portraitist. Both she and Elisabeth were accepted into the Académie Royale on the same day. Some considered the women as rivals, but there is no proof that they ever felt that they were in competition with each other.

enough money on her own; she didn't need a husband's support. Her artistic talents gave her an independence that many women of the time never had. But eventually, she changed her mind about Jean and they married on January 11, 1776.

That same year, Elisabeth received her first royal commission. She was asked to paint portraits of the King's Louis XVI's brother, the Count of Provence. Although these paintings no longer exist today, they must have been impressive, because an even bigger project came next. In 1778, Elisabeth received her first commission from Queen Marie Antoinette. She was asked to create a portrait of the queen based on four paintings that other artists had done. When Elisabeth finished the portrait, she was summoned to the palace at Versailles to paint Marie Antoinette's portrait from real life. It was exhibited at the Hotel de Lubert and is still known as one of the most famous paintings of the queen.

On February 12, 1780, Elisabeth gave birth to a daughter she named Jeanne Julie Louise. Slowing down during her pregnancy was not easy for the vivacious artist. In fact, she refused to step away from her easel until she went into labor.

Being a mother didn't stop Elisabeth's active social life.

Elisabeth was friends with stage actors, musicians, writers, and intellectuals. Every week, she held a musical and literary gathering at her home. Many felt privileged to be invited. Elisabeth was a charming person who loved being around people. That may be why she painted them so well. And others liked being around her because of her intelligence and her talent. Her reputation as a fine portraitist grew. She was far more talented and had more experience than most male portraitists at the time. Still, the members of the Académie Royale wouldn't let her join. Elisabeth wanted to join the Académie because besides being prestigious, it would give her the opportunity to exhibit at their Salon, held every two years.

Working for royalty gave Elisabeth some powerful friends. In 1783, Marie Antoinette gave a royal command to the Académie, demanding that her favorite artist, Elisabeth, be admitted as a member. After years of being excluded, Elisabeth was proud to be a member of this influential group, even if she had needed help to make it happen. Finally, she could show her paintings at the Académie's Salon. Over the next four years, she exhibited more than forty paintings there. As a member of the Académie, Elisabeth's career skyrocketed. She spent most of her time painting and discussing art.

But frightening times were ahead. The late-eighteenth century was the beginning of the French Revolution, and France was in turmoil. The French people no longer believed in the old regime, with the monarchy running the country. They wanted more power for the people; they wanted big changes. Marie Antoinette and her husband, Louis XVI, were losing what popularity they once had. Citizens thought the queen was frivolous and wasted their money. They also suspected she was a spy for Austria, her country of birth. The queen commissioned a portrait of herself with her children, hoping it would show her as a good mother and queen. However, the finished painting was not very flattering, and Marie Antoinette was outraged. Looks

18

and appearance were very important to her, and everyone knew it.
To do work that wasn't exactly what
Her Majesty wanted was disrespect-
ful. The queen knew that Elisabeth
was the only artist who could make
her happy. And so, Elisabeth created *Marie Antoinette and Her
Children* in 1787. Elisabeth's painting showed Marie Antoinette in a
vibrant red dress, with a baby in
her lap and her other two children
at her sides. It was exactly what
Marie Antoinette had wanted and

*Marie Antoinette
and Her Children*

she was very pleased.
The painting still
hangs in the palace
at Versailles today.

As a friend of
the queen, Elisabeth
thought the royal
family should stay in
power. After all, her
career had flourished
under the monar-
chy system. But her
reputation started to
suffer, not because of
her art, but because
of her political ties.
The media began
to attack her and
accused her of having
affairs with powerful

Self-portrait with Daughter, 1789

> "All I have endured convinces me that my only happiness has been in painting."
> —Elisabeth Vigée Le Brun

men, which she strongly denied. People threatened her and her family and vandalized their home. There was nightly violence in the streets of France. Elisabeth couldn't concentrate on her art with the threat of danger in the air.

Taking her daughter and a governess, Elisabeth fled from France in 1789. A mob of Parisian citizens had just stormed the royal palace at Versailles. Elisabeth was afraid for her life and knew she would die if she stayed. Her husband stayed behind to look after his business.

Self-portrait in a Straw Hat, 1792

Away from her home country, with no regular commissions, Elisabeth had to start over again and begin a new stage in her career. No one could deny her talent and experience, and she began to work again. For the next twelve years, she worked in Italy, Austria, Germany, and Russia. In 1790, she exhibited a self-portrait at the Uffizi museum in Florence. All who saw the portrait praised and admired it.

> Today, you can find Elisabeth's paintings in some of the world's greatest museums, such as the Louvre in Paris, the Metropolitan Museum of Art in New York, and the National Gallery of Art in Washington. One of Elisabeth's paintings is also in the private collection of Queen Elizabeth II, in Windsor Castle, England.

After three years of living away from home, Elisabeth wanted to return to Paris, but she couldn't. Her name, along with the names of others who had left France during the violence of the Revolution, was added to a list of *émigrés* — people who have to leave a country for political reasons. When the new regime took power, the people on that list lost all their rights as French citizens. Although her husband asked the Revolutionary government many times to take Elisabeth's name off the list, he couldn't help. By 1794, it got too dangerous for Jean to even be associated with his wife in political exile. He sued for divorce, which was granted.

Elisabeth didn't wallow in her personal problems. She found comfort in her art, and continued to paint and exhibit throughout Europe. In 1795, she traveled to Saint Petersburg, Russia, and was commissioned to paint portraits for the royal family. Two of her paintings were even sent to Paris from Russia and exhibited, but the artist was still not permitted to accompany her work.

During the years in exile, Elisabeth became a really smart business woman. She had to learn it all herself, with no mentor or husband to advise her. With her strong reputation, she discovered she could charge prices for her portraits that were higher than what most male artists charged. She even created a price list. The cost depended on what the customer wanted in the portrait (a bust only, the whole body, a number of people). She earned quite a large fortune.

In Paris in 1799, a group of eight artists gave a petition to the government in favor of letting Elisabeth return to France. It was signed by 255 writers, artists, and scientists. In 1800, her name was permanently removed from the list of *émigrés*, and she was allowed to enter her birth country again. Elisabeth was smart with the money she'd made from her commissions in other countries, and had invested it very carefully so she could afford to support herself in a comfortable lifestyle. When she returned to France, she bought a country house in the Louveciennes and an apartment in Paris.

As Elisabeth grew older, her painting slowed down, but her social life didn't. Many people continued to visit her art studio to have great conversations and look at the beautiful artwork. She died in Paris at the age of eighty-seven.

Although Elisabeth Vigée Le Brun was conservative in her politics, she was a revolutionary woman. As a self-taught painter, she supported herself throughout her entire sixty-year career. You can see her work today in leading museums all over the world. Through her great portraits, Elisabeth created a portrait of herself that has gone down in history: a successful painter whose passion for art was greater than any obstacle that stood in her way.

> You can see many of Elisabeth's paintings online, at websites such as The Art of Elisabeth Louise Vigée Le Brun at **www.batguano.com/vigee.html.**

EMILY CARR

1871 - 1945

WILD AT HEART

The pressure to fit in can be hard to bear. We are always hearing what we are supposed to do and how we are supposed to act, but it's our differences that make us special. Canadian artist Emily Carr had to deal with these pressures all her life — and for all her life she refused to follow convention. She chose to follow her own heart instead. Although it took many years for Emily Carr's work to earn recognition and praise, she never gave up. She continued to make art she truly believed in and she chased her dreams until she caught them.

Emily was born on December 13, 1871, in Victoria, British Columbia. The small, quiet city on the southern tip of Vancouver Island was named after Queen Victoria and had a very English feel. Because Emily's father, Richard, had immigrated to Canada from England, this suited him just fine. The Carr family lived in a nice, big house with a large, well-kept garden.

Richard Carr owned a successful dry goods store. He and his wife, Emily, brought up their nine children (little Emily was the eighth child) to be proper young ladies and gentlemen. Or at least they tried to bring them up that way. Richard wanted his girls to be prim and polite and take their religious studies very seriously.

Emily (or Millie, her childhood nickname) was a lot different from her older sisters. She loved to ride her pony, Johnny, through the rugged woods and to the beach near their house. Emily never rode sidesaddle, as ladies were supposed to, because she could go much faster with a leg on each side of the pony. She loved to splash in the mud and run and jump until her little legs felt like they might fall off. But most of all, Emily loved animals — from the birds whose songs woke her in the morning to the tiny chipmunks that scurried between the trees, Emily always felt a special bond with animals. She even enjoyed hanging out with the family cow, stroking her soft neck and looking into her pretty brown eyes.

Emily's energy was so boundless that her family, although they loved her free spirit, considered her a bit of problem child. She was often scolded for her bad behavior, but scolding and punishments didn't bother Emily much, because she knew that she was only truly happy being herself. She simply couldn't pretend to be proper when she was really wild at heart.

The only time Emily sat still was when she was drawing, which was her favorite pastime. When she was about eight years old, she drew a picture of Richard's dog and gave it to him. He thought the picture was so excellent that he enrolled Emily in drawing classes. At the time, drawing and sketching were considered ladylike hobbies, so the Carrs encouraged Emily in her studies. No one dreamed you could make a career of art — especially if you were a woman.

In 1886, Emily's mother died of tuberculosis, a contagious lung disease. Just two years later, while the children were still grieving their mother's loss, their father passed away. At sixteen, Emily had to grow up quickly. She wasn't quite ready to be on her own yet, though, and so her strict oldest sister, Edith, ran the household. The Carr children also had a family guardian — an adult family friend who watched over the money in their bank account and made sure they had everything they needed. When Emily asked for Edith's permission to go to Europe to study art, the answer was a stern, "No." Since that didn't satisfy Emily, she asked the family guardian instead, and eventually persuaded him to let her go art college in San Francisco, California. At her new school, Emily learned basic techniques for drawing and painting, all the while dreaming of becoming a famous artist. But perhaps just as important, Emily learned to be away from her family and to take care of herself.

When she returned from San Francisco in 1893, Emily opened the Carr home to local children and gave them art lessons in the dining room. Lesson time was full of laughter and fun. After her classes, the place was usually quite a mess, so Emily turned the barn into a big art studio and held lessons there. The barn was bright with high ceilings and smelled like fresh hay and apples.

After a year of teaching, Emily had her first art show at the Victoria Fall Fair. She was

> Emily Carr's childhood house was built from California redwood trees in 1863 and is still standing today at 207 Government Street in Victoria, British Columbia.

25

pleased, but thought of it as only a small success. How would she become a great artist and improve her painting if she stayed in the same place her whole life? She yearned for adventure. So in 1899, when she was invited by a friend to spend a few months among the Nootka People in Ucluelet, British Columbia, she agreed without hesitating.

Although she couldn't speak their language, Emily fit in immediately with the Nootka. To communicate with them, she used big gestures, strong facial expressions, and smiled at everyone she met. Soon, the Nootka gave Emily a special nickname, *Klee Wyck*, which means "Laughing One," because she was always in such high spirits.

In Ucluelet, Emily concentrated on her art. The Nootka people inspired her. Yet at the same time, she was saddened because she saw that their culture was in danger of disappearing. Some Nootka children went to boarding schools where they were forbidden to speak their own language or practice their religion. Emily wanted to capture as much of their proud history as she could in her art, so she painted her new friends in their everyday lives. Totem poles (traditional sculptures, usually of one or many animals, to represent a family's spirit) captivated Emily especially. She had never seen art so colorful and so powerful, and she painted many totem poles during her stay with the Nootka.

Not long after returning home, Emily left again, this time to study art in England. The journey across the ocean was long and difficult, but she arrived safely. She enrolled in the Westminster Art School in London, but it turned out that big city was no place for someone who drew so much inspiration from nature. She hated the crowds, the smog, the constant noise, and the busy lifestyle. Unfortunately, she didn't like her art classes much better. Instead of painting with bold colrs and strong images in the new style she had started to cultivate since her stay with the Nootka, Emily's teachers wanted her to paint realistically, in a traditional style. Of course, such an independent woman resented being told what and how to paint.

Emily's body couldn't handle the stress or pressure of the city and she fell ill in the fall of 1902. She spent more than a year recovering in hospital. Under strict orders from the doctor, Emily was forbidden to even hold a paintbrush. But she kept herself occupied in other ways: She raised a family of songbirds and sketched whenever she felt strong enough.

The return to Canada energized Emily. She earned money by drawing clever cartoons for a local newspaper and teaching art at a Vancouver women's club. In 1907, Emily and her sister Alice went on a cruise to Alaska, where she visited Totem Walk at Sitka, a path lined with trees and totem poles. Emily's mission was to paint as many of the majestic sculptures as possible.

Next, Emily set her sights on France, and journeyed there with Alice in 1910. She had heard that French artists were using dramatic colors and painting in new styles that were very different from the traditional styles. Her friend, English artist Henry Phelan Gibb, took her to the French countryside, where she painted landscape pictures such as *Autumn in France*, in 1911. Much to her delight, the Salon d'Automne, a Paris art gallery, even exhibited two of her paintings.

Emily felt ready to return home and show everyone what she had learned in Europe. In 1912, she moved to Vancouver and held an exhibition of her work. The people who came to see it had a mixed response. Some critics praised the way she used color so freely, but others thought her paintings were too "modern" looking and dismissed them.

Negative opinions didn't stop Emily from painting what she wanted in her own unique style. That same year she left Vancouver, taking with her only her art supplies, some blankets, and food. She traveled by boat to the villages of more than fifteen aboriginal peoples in northern British Columbia. Feeling

Emily Carr

a need to capture the lives of the native people, Emily sketched and painted the scenery and the villagers. She wanted to document their way of life and worked so intensely it was as if she couldn't stop. By the end of her journey she'd produced more than two hundred pieces of art.

Emily had the same hopes as other artists — to have her paintings exhibited for the public. She approached the government in Victoria and suggested they put her work on display in the parliament buildings. She explained that her paintings showing the province's First Nations' culture would benefit all who saw them. People would learn something about Canadian history when they saw her paintings. The government officials considered her idea at first, but turned her down when they saw the paintings. They said they were too vibrant and unrealistic.

And so, without any government support, Emily held her own exhibition once again. Just as before, the reviews weren't all good. Only a few paintings sold, which disappointed Emily because she was hoping to make enough money to continue living in her studio and focusing on her art. That plan would have to wait, because she was broke.

> Emily received two marriage proposals in her life, but she felt strongly that her art came first, and didn't want to be tied down to a husband. She never once regretted her decision.

Even though Emily was tough, she couldn't help but feel hurt by all the rejection. But she hadn't yet run out of ideas that would allow her to spend her days painting. Emily had inherited a piece of land from her father, and on it she built a house, which she named Hill House. She divided the structure into four living areas and she hoped to have tenants move in. She planned to live off the rent money they would pay and spend her days painting. Being a landlady couldn't be that hard, she thought.

But everything that could go wrong did go wrong. Emily had a hard time finding people to rent the apartments, and when she did the tenants paid only very low rents. Emily even rented out her own apartment and moved up to the attic, but she still struggled financially. Not only did she have no money, she had no time, because some of her tenants were very demanding. They constantly interrupted Emily every time she picked up her paintbrush. The only thing that saved her during this difficult time was her love of animals. She raised and sold English sheepdogs (called Bobtails), hens, and rabbits. She also made hand-painted pottery and sold it to tourists.

Emily hadn't given up on art, but the stress of making money zapped her creative energy. In ten years, she managed to complete only about twenty small paintings. Also, she knew that her neighbors gossiped about her. Emily's life must have seemed very odd to most people. She had never married (which was considered strange at the time), lived with lots of animals, and even had a pet Javanese monkey named Woo. She wore funny hats and dresses that were too big for her. She used a baby carriage to transport her groceries and art supplies and was always accompanied by a parade of animals. And to top it all off, she considered herself an artist at a time when some people thought that only men could make great art. But Emily didn't care what people said, because she'd always stood out and let her individuality shine through.

In 1927, Emily received an unexpected visitor. Eric Brown was the director of the National Gallery of Canada in Ottawa.

> Emily always signed her work "M. Emily Carr." She used the M to set herself apart from her sisters Edith and Elizabeth, and also to represent Millie, her childhood nickname.

He wasn't bothered by the dogs that barked at him when he arrived or by the way Emily hung chairs from the ceiling of her studio. He'd heard about Emily's work and had come to see it for himself. Eric was so impressed with Emily's talent that he arranged to have the works of art shipped to the National Gallery for the "Exhibition of Canadian West Coast Art — Native and Modern." On the train ride to Ottawa, Emily couldn't hide her excitement. She

> "Be careful that you do not write or paint anything that is not your own, that you don't know in your own soul."
> —Emily Carr

also felt worried. What if, like at previous exhibitions, her work wasn't understood and her talent rejected?

To calm her fears, Emily spent some time with other artists, the well-known Group of Seven in Toronto, which included famous artists such as A.Y. Jackson, Edwin Holgate, and Arthur Lismer. They painted in a new and bold style, and immediately understood Emily's creative vision. Lawren Harris was the Group member who particularly encouraged Emily, and she in turn admired his work. They became lifelong friends and in the years to come exchanged hundreds of letters, sharing their views about art and being an artist.

Thanks to the success of the exhibition and the contact with other artists, Emily's passion to paint burned brighter than ever. She began to paint again, this time using even stronger, cleaner lines and more powerful images. She explored Cubism (a style from Europe in which artists painted objects as though they were broken up into different shapes and put back together again in what seems like a random way) and journeyed again to Native communities in the north. By 1930, her work had been exhibited in Toronto, Montreal, Seattle, and Washington, DC. She even gave lectures on modern art that captivated her audiences. In just about three years, Emily had gone from chasing her dream to living it. Emily's work finally received the acclaim it deserved.

But success couldn't change Emily or the things she loved — painting, traveling, and her animals. For the next eleven years, until 1942, Emily took off to the wilderness twice a year and only painted for weeks at a time. She bought a trailer that she loved so much, she practically considered it one of her animals, and called it The Elephant. By attaching The Elephant to a truck to move it, she made camp wherever her heart desired. She felt completely free.

Gradually, the influence of Emily's childhood in rugged British Columbia became more obvious in her work. Trees were an especially important subject to her, and as she grew older she felt a stronger connection with nature. She would escape with her little caravan of animals and paint mighty trees, using earth tones and vibrant greens. Emily's work continued to be exhibited in Canada and abroad. She was especially proud of

The Emily Carr Institue of Art and Design in Vancouver, British Columbia

her exhibition at the Tate Gallery in London, England, because when she was younger she never thought the British would understand her work. The Vancouver Art Gallery also gave Emily her very own art show, as did the Dominion Gallery in Montreal.

As her art began to succeed, her health began to fail. Emily had her first heart attack in 1937, and although she didn't let it slow her down, gradually her body couldn't handle the traveling and she moved in with her sister Alice, who helped take care of her.

When she wasn't painting, Emily was writing. She had kept a journal for most of her life, but in the years after her struggles to succeed, she wrote more seriously. One collection

Emily Carr's gravestone, Victoria, British Columbia

of stories about her experiences visiting First Nations villages was published as *Klee Wyck* in 1941. It won a Governor General's award that year (the highest honor for Canadian literature at the time). She also published *The Book of Small*, about her childhood memories.

In early 1945, when she was in her early seventies, Emily got great news. The University of British Columbia was going to present her with an honorary doctorate at the spring graduation ceremony, to recognize her contributions to Canadian art and culture. Emily had never cared what others thought, but finally being appreciated made her feel proud.

A few weeks before she was to receive the degree, Emily Carr passed away in Victoria. Thankfully, her independent spirit and her love of Canada still live on in her work. Even today, she is considered one of Canada's most famous artists, and her life reminds us that chasing a dream is always worth the effort.

> Visit the gallery section of the website Emily Carr at Home and at Work (**www.emilycarr.ca**) to learn more about Emily and to see some of her paintings.

Georgia O'Keeffe

1887 - 1986

THROUGH THE EYES OF AN ARTIST

At a time when almost no women were artists, let alone were able to make a living from art, Georgia O'Keeffe's unique view of the world captured America's imagination. Her special gift was showing people the beauty in everyday objects. She allowed the world to experience what it was like to see through her eyes. Georgia O'Keeffe is known still as one of America's greatest painters.

Georgia Totto O'Keeffe was born on a dairy farm in Sun Prairie, Wisconsin, on November 15, 1887. Her father, Frank, was an Irish immigrant, and her mother, Ida, the daughter of a Hungarian count. They already had one child, Francis Jr., before Georgia was born. In the next few years, their family continued to grow. They had four more daughters and one more son.

Life on the farm was never boring. If Georgia didn't have chores to do, such as weeding the vegetable garden, cleaning the house, or helping to prepare meals, she was busy just enjoying her beautiful surroundings. She knew the names of all the wildflowers and could identify birds by their songs. Rather than playing with her brothers and sisters, Georgia preferred to spend a lot of time alone. She could sit in the shade of a tree for hours, amusing herself with her homemade dollhouse. She also loved to sit outside and draw pictures.

When she was five years old, Georgia started at the local one-room schoolhouse, called Town Hall School. From the start, Georgia didn't like that school. The students had to learn by memorizing, while Georgia preferred thinking things through for herself.

Ida insisted that her children, especially her daughters, attend school. Ida once wanted to be a doctor, but gave up her dream to raise her family. She wanted her children to get a good education so they could choose their own paths in life. As well as regular school, Georgia and two of her younger sisters took private art lessons at home. They practiced drawing different shapes and spent hours copying the works of famous artists out of books.

Georgia's natural artistic talent shone through right away. Her family thought that she might grow up to become an art teacher. Hardly any women made their living as artists at the time. But Georgia didn't let that stop her and announced that she was, in fact, going to be an artist.

When she was fourteen years old, Georgia went to the Sacred Heart Academy in the state capital of Madison. Being away from home was difficult, but she adjusted to her new life, and took her art classes very seriously. One day, her art teacher criticized a drawing Georgia had made of a baby's hand, because she'd only used small, dark lines. Georgia had never thought of drawing large pictures with long, free lines, but the idea was appealing. She tried it and never used the small, heavy lines again.

When Georgia started high school in Milwaukee in 1902, her art teacher brought in a flower for the class to draw. Georgia found that drawing something from real life, instead of copying from a book, suited her much better.

The O'Keeffes moved to Virginia that same year, because they wanted to live somewhere warmer. Georgia enrolled at the Chatham Episcopal Institute, which was a private school for girls. She was quite popular there, and everyone knew her because she was different from other students. Everyone called her the "queen of the art studio." She dressed in very plain clothes and wore her hair in a simple style, pulled back off her face. Elizabeth May Willis taught art at Chatham and let Georgia use the art room whenever she wanted. Elizabeth gave Georgia a special art award when she graduated at the age of seventeen and even encouraged her to continue studying at the Art Institute of Chicago.

Georgia felt fortunate to spend her days studying and creating art in Chicago and really enjoyed her new classes, but still she felt something was missing. She was learning traditional art techniques of the European masters, but she wondered about new, younger artists. Georgia worked hard. Every month, the students' work was put on display and ranked from best to worst by teachers at the Institute. After a few months, Georgia's work was first in the class.

In 1906, Georgia got sick with typhoid fever and had to return home to recover. It was a frightening time because she nearly died. She was too ill to go back to Chicago that September, but when she grew stronger, she enrolled at the

Art Students League in New York City. She still wanted to study art and knew that the Art Students League had the reputation of letting its pupils experiment with new and different techniques, instead of mostly focusing on classical

> "I found I could say things with color and shapes that I couldn't say in any other way — things I had no words for."
> —Georgia O'Keeffe

styles. Also, the school in New York encouraged cooperation among students, rather than the heavy competition that the Art Institute supported.

Being in New York was thrilling for the young artist. She got along well with her fellow students, and she sometimes agreed to pose while they painted her portrait. Georgia really liked her teachers, too. Her favorite teacher was William Merritt Chase. When he walked into the classroom, all the students fell silent — he had such a strong presence. He made them paint a new picture every day and encouraged them to use lots of color and strong lines. At the end of the school year, William awarded Georgia a $100 prize for her still-life picture of a rabbit and a copper pot.

In 1908 Georgia and her friends went to see an exhibit of new drawings by Auguste Rodin, a French sculptor, at a gallery called the 291. The owner of the gallery was Alfred Stieglitz, a famous photographer. Georgia was impressed with the way Alfred talked about the drawings, but she felt too shy to speak to him herself.

During this time, the O'Keeffe family had serious money problems. Frank's business wasn't doing well and he could no longer afford Georgia's tuition. Plus, Ida was ill with tuberculosis and the whole family was worried. Only twenty-one years old, Georgia moved to Chicago and got a job as an advertising illustrator. The work wasn't fun or creative, but at least she earned a paycheck. But when Georgia fell ill with the

A photo portrait of Georgia O'Keeffe taken by Alfred Stieglitz, 1918

measles, she had to quit her job and return home to recover. She wondered if she would ever paint again.

In 1912, Georgia was depressed and uncertain of her future when her old teacher, Elizabeth, contacted her. Elizabeth asked Georgia to teach an art class at Chatham, and Georgia accepted. She also became a student again by taking an advanced painting class for teachers at the University of Virginia. Her teacher, Alon Bement, believed in a new kind of art. He taught his class about composition — how to make every part of a painting balance with the other parts — and how to paint with simple lines and shapes. Also, he didn't believe that all paintings had to be real; he thought abstract art, which expresses feelings but doesn't necessarily look like a real object, was a valuable art form. Georgia felt inspired by his new ideas. She began to experiment with the new style while continuing to teach to support herself.

In 1916, Georgia sent some charcoal drawings to her friend Anita Pollitzer in New York City. Anita knew they were special, and took them to Alfred Stieglitz, at the 291 gallery. He was blown away by the drawings, and immediately exhibited them. When Georgia found out, she was enraged that he had not asked her permission. She traveled to New York, determined to give Alfred a piece of her mind. But when Alfred told her how much he

Georgia sent this charcoal piece, *Drawing XIII*, to Alfred Stieglitz in 1915.

loved the drawings, Georgia was no longer angry. Eventually, the two became friends. Georgia's first solo show took place at the 291 gallery the following year.

In the fall of that same year Georgia took a teaching job near Amarillo, Texas. She loved the rugged landscape, and spent hours exploring the canyons and painting. During this time, she exchanged many letters with Alfred. He was married, but he and his wife were separated. Georgia and Alfred became closer over time and soon, they fell in love.

Georgia O'Keeffe was a feminist who believed that women should have the freedom to choose any career they wanted. In 1914, she joined the National Women's Party and was a member for thirty years. She strongly supported women's right to vote in elections, a right that women were granted in 1920.

Alfred Stieglitz photographing Georgia O'Keeffe at Lake George, 1924

Once again, Georgia fell ill, this time with the flu. Alfred insisted that she move to New York to get well and paint full time. She resisted at first, but devoting all her time to her art was what she'd always dreamed of doing. In 1918, Georgia moved back to New York and in with Alfred. With Alfred's help, she found a patron and set to work.

The 1920s were productive for Georgia. She was developing her own unique style as an artist. She began to use flowers as the subjects of her paintings, and she would paint them from very close up, so they looked the way a tiny insect might see them. She didn't want to paint the flowers realistically. Rather, she wanted to show viewers how she felt about flowers. In 1923, she had a solo show at the Anderson Galleries in New York, and thousands of people went to see her work. Georgia sold quite a few paintings, even though it was sometimes hard for her to part with her work because it was so personal to her.

Georgia was feeling good about herself and her work, so whenever Alfred brought up the subject of marriage, she usually didn't want to discuss it. Her life was going well, she loved Alfred, and she didn't feel that marrying him would change anything. Besides, he was older by twenty-four years. But Alfred was persistent and he clearly loved her very much, so eventually she changed her mind. On December 11, 1924, Georgia and Alfred were married.

Georgia's career was really taking off. Critics praised her work and she sold many paintings. She was the sensation of the American art scene. In 1928, she sold a series of calla lily paintings to a French collector for $25,000. Such a high price was practically unheard of at the time, especially for paintings done by a woman. Because women were generally not respected as artists, their work wasn't valued as highly as the work of male artists.

Although the newlyweds had art in common, they were still very different. Their differences caused many arguments.

Alfred was always entertaining guests while Georgia needed a lot of time alone to work. Also, Alfred only wanted to be in New York City or at his house on Lake George in New York State, but Georgia longed to travel. She had painted too many skyscrapers and landscapes and wanted to find new inspiration for her work.

A trip to Taos, New Mexico, lifted her spirits. Something about the scenery spoke to Georgia in a way she'd never known before, and she moved back and forth between Lake Taos, New Mexico, and New York. She stayed with friends, painted views of mountains and deserts, and hiked across the unspoiled

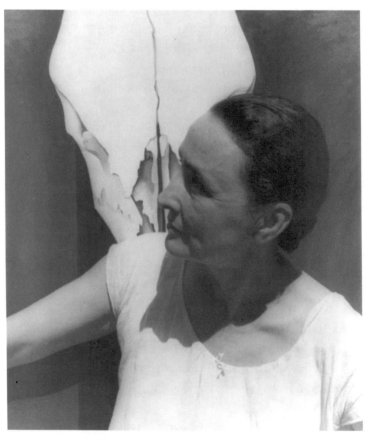

Georgia O'Keeffe in New York, 1936

landscape. During one of her hikes, Georgia was struck by something that changed her art. She found animal bones lying in the desert. Georgia thought the bones, bleached dazzling white from the sun, were beautiful. She collected them and shipped them to New York to paint them. Sometimes she painted bones next to flowers or feathers, and she even used them to decorate her home.

> "When you take a flower in your hand and really look at it, it's your world for the moment. I want to give that world to someone else. Most people in the city rush around so, they have no time to look at a flower. I want them to see it whether they want to or not." —Georgia O'Keeffe

Georgia made many friends in New Mexico, such as novelist D.H. Lawrence and photographer Ansel Adams. Georgia's face must have inspired Ansel as it inspired her classmates so many years before, because he took many beautiful photographs of her. When she wasn't in New York, she'd ship her work to Alfred, who organized exhibitions. The critics' reviews of Georgia's bone paintings were mixed at first. Some critics thought they were creepy. But eventually they were accepted as inspired works of art.

In the meantime, the tension in Georgia and Alfred's relationship got worse. He worried about her when she wasn't in New York, and Georgia found it stressful living in two places and having two lives at the same time. Also the pressure on Georgia to produce paintings that the critics and art dealers would like took its toll on her. She had a nervous breakdown in 1933.

It took many months for Georgia to feel like herself again, and she didn't paint at all during her recovery. When she got better, she went back to New Mexico. She stayed at a place called the Ghost Ranch and began painting again. But Georgia felt that she wanted a place of her very own rather than renting

Georgia O'Keeffe in New Mexico, 1950

other people's property, so she bought an adobe house (made with a type of clay) at Abiquiu for $6,000. It had no running water or electricity. Later on Georgia bought a second home in the same area with all the modern conveniences.

Alfred died of a stroke on July 13, 1946. He was eighty-two years old. Georgia tried to be strong, but to her close friends she talked about how much she missed him, and how sad she felt. After Alfred's death, Georgia moved to New Mexico for good.

Because she no longer had to spend part of the year in New York and she was making a lot of money from her art, Georgia began to travel the world in the 1950s. She went to Europe, South America, and Africa. Georgia loved the view of rivers and fields as she flew over them in a plane, and she painted these aerial views.

One morning in 1971, Georgia woke up to the shock of her life. Everything looked blurry. Confused by what could be wrong with her eyes, George sought medical help. Doctors told her that her vision would be like that for the rest of her life. Georgia's eyesight was so precious to her she couldn't imagine living without seeing the sights that inspired her every day. She fell into a depression.

Thankfully, a friend helped Georgia through this difficult time. Juan Hamilton was a young potter who worked at odd jobs around Georgia's home. They became close, and Georgia gave him advice about his career. He encouraged Georgia to paint again, which she did. Assistants helped her to mix colors.

Until the end of her life, Georgia continued to create art. Many people came to see her in the desert. They were intrigued by the famous artist who rarely appeared in public. Sometimes she invited people in with open arms; sometimes she told them to get lost. It all depended on her mood. Georgia felt that she had earned the right to her privacy.

45

Georgia O'Keeffe passed away on March 6, 1986. She always said that she wanted to live to be one hundred years old. At ninety-eight, she came pretty close. Georgia left behind a lifetime of art that today you can see in some of the most famous museums in the United States. She had a special vision, and she never stopped trying to share it with the world.

The Georgia O'Keeffe Museum in Santa Fe, New Mexico, has many of Georgia's paintings in its permanent collection. You can see some of them on the museum's website at **www.okeeffemuseum.org.**

LOUISE NEVELSON

1899 - 1988

A PASSION TO SUCCEED

You've probably heard the expression, "If at first you don't succeed, try, try again," but living by that saying isn't easy. Life often holds disappointments, and things don't always work out as we plan them. Louise Nevelson lived through many disappointments, but she never let them discourage her from pursuing art. She believed in herself and persevered to become one of the greatest American sculptors of the twentieth century.

Louise Berliawsky was born on September 23, 1899, in the city of Kiev, Russia. Her father, Isaac, worked selling lumber. Her mother, Minna, worked at home raising Louise and her older brother, Nathan.

The Berliawsky family was Jewish and faced many hardships because of their religion. Anti-Semitism (the persecution of Jewish people) was common in Russia, which made the lives of Jewish people almost unbearable at times. Isaac had problems finding sellers and buyers for his lumber, because no one wanted to deal with a Jew. And when he did do business, he was often cheated out of a lot of money. He also feared that his family would be hurt or killed in a *pogrom*, which was a planned attack on Jewish people, where synagogues were burned and Jews were beaten to death.

When Louise was three years old, her parents had another baby, Anita. Thinking of his growing family's future, Isaac knew he had to get his wife and children to the United States, away from the violence and danger. In 1902, he left for America. When he had made enough money, he would send for the rest of his family. Louise was too young to understand her father's plan. She was so sad without him that she refused to speak for six months.

For the next two years, Louise, her mother, and her siblings lived with their grandparents in the village of Shushnecky. Louise thought about her father often, dreaming of the day he would send for her. Just before her sixth birthday, he did. Minna and her children took a steamship to the United States.

The Berliawskys were back together again in Rockland, Maine, a busy little town on the east coast. They had a house, and Isaac's new business, working in lumber and construction, was going very well. In 1906, they had another child, named Lillian.

But moving to a strange country wasn't easy. Few Jews lived in Rockland, and although Louise quickly learned to speak English, she never truly felt that she fit in. Every year, Rockland picked a girl to be Miss Lobster and ride through town in a parade. Louise knew she would never be picked. She was just too different. She didn't have many friends, and her family was the most important thing in the world to her.

At school, Louise never got great marks. She didn't care for spelling or math lessons, but she excelled at art class. Drawing and painting and creating with her hands made her happy and made her forget that she was lonely. She was always creating art, even at home, where every few weeks she rearranged the living room furniture in a new, fun way. Soon, instead of calling her by her name, teachers and students simply called Louise "the artist." Louise also took dance lessons, singing lessons, and piano lessons. Her parents encouraged her artistic talents. They wished her grades were better, but they could tell that Louise's life would never be ordinary, and that her creativity made her special.

By the time she was nine, Louise was telling everyone that she was going to be a sculptor. She couldn't explain how she knew, she just felt it. In high school, she focused most of her energy on the arts. She also participated in school activities such as the basketball team and the glee club (a singing group), but she still felt different from other teenagers. And even though anti-Semitism wasn't as strong in the United States as in Russia, some students called her names and made fun of her for being Jewish.

Between school and art, Louise also worked part-time as a secretary in a lawyer's office. Through her job, she met a man named Charles Nevelson. He was a Russian Jew like Louise, but he was fifteen years older and very rich. He lived in sophisticated New York City, and he invited Louise to go there to meet his family. Louise had never seen so many people and tall buildings, and she loved New York immediately.

Louise agreed to marry Charles, on a few conditions. She told him that she was going to be a great artist, and that she wouldn't be the type of wife who stayed home all the time. She had to have freedom to study and create art. Charles told her that he encouraged her artistic work. They were married on June 12, 1920, and moved to New York.

When she wasn't taking art lessons, Louise loved to walk around the city and gaze at the amazing architecture. She was mostly free to do as she pleased, except sometimes when she had to visit Charles's family and friends. Louise found them snobbish and they didn't understand her passion for creating art. But her sister Anita visited a lot, and they spent entire days strolling through art galleries and museums. Louise

Louise,
shortly after
her 1920
marriage

dreamed about the day when her work would be displayed in a museum.

In February 1922, Louise's life changed in a big way. She gave birth to a son, Mike Nevelson, and fell into postpartum depression (a deep sadness that some new mothers feel after having a baby). She wondered how she could be an artist and a mother at the same time. She wondered if she could even be a good mother at all.

> "I did not become anything, I was an artist. Early in school, they called me 'the artist.' When teachers wanted things painted, they called upon me, they called up 'the artist.' I am not saying that I learned my name… I am saying that they learned it."
> —Louise Nevelson

To keep the sadness away, Louise pursued art and music with more enthusiasm than ever. She even studied Eastern philosophies. Although Charles claimed to be supportive of her artistic activities, he thought she was taking things too far. He wanted her to be home more often and to be more normal. He hated how Louise dressed in flashy outfits that made other people stare (she would even make dresses out of colorful table napkins, if she liked the pattern).

Her husband's objections didn't bother Louise, especially after 1926, when Louise saw a painting by Pablo Picasso for the first time. She learned that he painted in a style called cubism, in which the artist paints a subject using geometric shapes like cubes and triangles, instead of painting the subject realistically. Cubism was a style of modern art that Louise had been waiting to discover. She started full-time classes at the Art Students League in 1929, hoping to learn more about it.

Louise learned that one of the world's best modern art teachers was Hans Hofmann. He had pioneered many artistic theories and techniques, and was a great mentor to hundreds of young artists. Louise was determined to study with him. However, Hans lived in Germany, which was a dangerous

Louise herself usually looked like a dramatic work of art. She wore colorful headscarfs, flowing peasant skirts, denim workshirts, and big necklaces that she made herself. She also wore up to five pairs of false eyelashes at once.

country for Jewish people at the time. The Nazi party and its leader, Adolf Hitler, were becoming very popular in Germany. Hitler and the Nazis preached hatred of Jewish people and wanted to destroy them. By the time World War II was over in 1945, the Nazis had killed more than six million Jews. But in 1931, Louise was not yet fully aware of the risks. She ignored Charles's demands that she stay in the U.S. and left for Germany. Her parents took care of Mike while she was away.

Louise had never been so excited about a class, but the experience was a huge disappointment. Hans Hofmann was Jewish, and he was so preoccupied with trying to leave Germany for the United States that he ignored his art class. He shut his school down only a few months after Louise arrived, and so she traveled around Europe before returning home. Despite the letdown, she became even more inspired by the works of European painters such as Henri Matisse.

In 1932, Louise and Charles ended their marriage. They knew they had nothing in common except their son. Without a husband, Louise had to rely on only herself, and she knew she had to make it as an artist or else die trying. Hans Hofmann had moved to New York and was teaching art, so Louise enrolled in his class again. This time, he paid a lot of attention to her. He answered all her questions about cubism and taught her how to use the techniques. Louise also got a temporary job as an assistant to the famous Mexican muralist Diego Rivera (husband of artist Frida Kahlo) when he was working in New York.

The Great Depression of the 1930s was a tough time for everyone. Millions of people were unemployed. Few were interested in art when they could hardly afford to feed their families. Louise earned some money by teaching art classes at a local boys' club. Around this time, after taking some sculpture classes, she also

> "I never doubted that my life would fulfill itself... or I wouldn't have had the courage [to create art]. I hate the word 'compromise.' I knew that I needed to claim my total life."
> —Louise Nevelson

realized that sculpture was her true love. She created bold cubic sculptures out of clay and plaster and painted them different primary colors. She even won an honorable mention in the American Artists Congress show, but she was still an unknown artist.

By 1941, Louise couldn't stand it any longer: She worked so hard and had dozens and dozens of sculptures and paintings, and yet still no one took her seriously as an artist. Louise took matters into her own hands. She strode into the Nierendorf Gallery, which was famous for its modern art, and demanded that the owner, Karl Nierendorf, exhibit her work. Karl was impressed by her courage and went to her studio to see her work. He agreed to give her a solo show in three weeks' time. At her first exhibition, the critics praised Louise's work, but despite the good reviews, no one bought her work.

For Louise's next show at Nierendorf's, she experimented with a new kind of sculpture. She created art from old furniture, scrap lumber, even bits of wood she found on the streets. Again, she got some attention, but didn't sell any pieces. Another exhibit, this time at the Norlyst Gallery, was called *The Circus: The Clown Is the Center of His World*. Louise was even bolder in her art. She created five-foot tall (1.5-meter) sculptures made of colored lights and slabs of wood, which represented the different sides of a human's personality. Although she was getting recognition as an artist, once again not a single sculpture sold. Louise's work was bold and different from other art that was popular at the time, and the public was simply not ready to accept her vision.

Louise reached the breaking point. She believed in her art, so it was frustrating for her when others did not understand or appreciate her ideas. She took the sculptures from *The Circus* apart and burned them. She also burned a few hundred paintings and some other sculptures. Today, we only know what some of these pieces looked like through the photographs that remain.

The most difficult decade of Louise's life was probably the 1940s. On top of artistic frustrations, her mother died in 1943, her father died in 1946, and then Karl Nierendorf died in 1948. Not only had she lost both her parents, but in Karl she'd lost a great friend and someone who believed in her art. Louise inherited some money from her mother and used it to buy a home. She renovated a huge house on East 30th Street. She turned it into one giant work of art and filled it with sculptures. She planted mirrors and kitchen utensils in the backyard garden, and even put sculptures in the bathtubs.

Although Louise was now surrounded by art, she felt uninspired and sad. But her illness went beyond depression this time. Doctors discovered that she had a tumor in her pelvis. In 1948, she had surgery to remove it and began the healing process.

When she was strong again, Louise felt she needed a vacation, so she took Anita to Yucatan, Mexico, and Guatemala. Louise loved the geometry and the structure of the Mayan temples in Mexico. She felt at home among them. When she got back to the U.S., she started fresh and began to sculpt feverishly.

In the early 1950s, Louise worked as though she would never stop. She created sculptures of wood and ceramic, and also made many etchings. To make an etching, an artist carves a design on a metal plate and places the plate in acid to make the carved design more pronounced. After removing the plate, she spreads ink over the design and presses paper on it, which transfers the design to the paper.) Louise decided that since she never sold anything in her solo shows, she would join as many group exhibitions as she could. Whenever a gallery asked Louise to contribute a piece to a show, she said yes. She wanted as many people as possible to see her art.

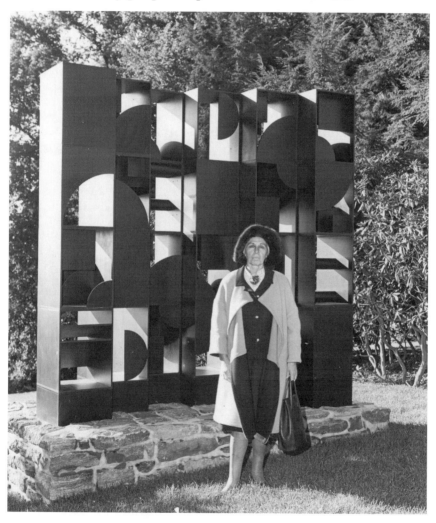

Louise Nevelson posed in front of her sculpture at Pocantico Hills, ca. 1969.

Her strategy worked. By 1955, the name Louise Nevelson was well known in the art world, and the Grand Central Moderns Gallery asked her to exhibit her work in a solo show that she called *Ancient Games and Ancient Places.* She held another exhibition, *Royal Voyage,* the following year, and *Moon Garden + One* in 1958. For these shows, Louise created what she called "environments," made up of many large sculptures. When people looked at the giant sculptures, they felt like they were in another world. She also painted every piece of the sculptures black, something for which she became known. Critics loved her work and called it "shocking" and "brilliant." Louise had finally become a major force in the art world.

When she was sixty, the Museum of Modern Art in New York invited Louise to take part in its *Sixteen Americans* exhibit. Her dream of showing her work in a museum had come true. Louise worked constantly for months, sleeping in her clothes and eating very little, to prepare a sculpture that would shock art viewers. She made *Dawn's Wedding Feast,* a 16-foot (5-meter) wall of boxes stacked one on top of the other and filled with chair legs, door knobs, wheels, and old tools. This time, everything was painted white. Louise wanted the giant environment to feel festive and used white to suggest a marriage celebration. The critics loved it.

From that point on, Louise had almost nothing but success. Her work was widely exhibited in respected galleries. She also continued to experiment with new materials — Plexiglass, aluminum, and steel became her new favorites.

Although Louise didn't normally agree to do commissioned work (when an artist gets paid to create a specific piece of art), she changed her mind, because she wanted people to see her art in all kinds of places, not just in museums. She created many sculptures for public spaces, such as *Atmosphere and Environment X* (1971) in Scottsdale, Arizona; *Sky Tree* (1977), a 54-foot (18-meter) sculpture that stands in San Francisco;

Louise Nevelson, surrounded by works in progress, in her studio, ca. 1975.

Dawn Shadows (1983) in Chicago; and *Night Sail* (1985) in Los Angeles. Six respected universities awarded her honorary degrees. She also received the best compliment possible, when a street in New York City — her favorite city in the world — was named Louise Nevelson Plaza.

Louise Nevelson passed away at her home in New York on April 17, 1988. She is remembered as one of the greatest sculptors of the twentieth century. Success never came easily, and for nearly forty years, she struggled to have her art noticed. Sometimes, she felt like giving up, but her drive to create art was so strong, and she believed in herself so much, that she never did. "I felt like a winner. And even if I didn't sell my work, I still felt like a winner. I am a winner," she said.

Louise Nevelson's work is permanently on display at the Museum of Modern Art (**www.moma.org**), and the Guggenheim Museum in New York City (**www.guggenheim.org**). Visit their websites to see some of her art.

FRIDA KAHLO

1907 - 1954

THE SOUL OF MEXICO

Great artists need to express themselves. They are usually passionate people who cannot keep their feelings bottled up. They use art as their way of sharing their feelings and views with the world. Mexican painter Frida Kahlo was passionate about all aspects of her life — her family, her political beliefs, and her feelings about her country. She faced many problems, such as painful illness and a terrible accident, that would leave most people discouraged and uninspired. But nothing could stop Frida Kahlo from sharing her love and passion through her art.

Magdalena Carmen Frida Kahlo was born on July 6, 1907, in Coyoacán, a town about an hour away from the hustle and bustle of Mexico City, the country's capital. Frida's father, Wilhelm Kahlo, was a German who changed his first name to Guillermo when he moved to Mexico at the age of nineteen. Frida's mother, Matilde Calderón, was a beautiful woman with exotic features. She was *Mestizo*, which is part Spanish and part Native Mexican. Frida was the third of the couple's four children. The family lived in an unusual, U-shaped house painted a brilliant blue.

Guillermo was a photographer who took pictures of buildings to document Mexico's unique architecture. He was also an amateur painter. Though he was a strict man, he had a special relationship with Frida, his favorite child.

Frida grew up during a difficult and frightening time in Mexico. For thirty-four years, a dictator named Porfirio Díaz had been president. He brought a lot of wealth to Mexico, but only for a small group of rich people. In 1910, poor citizens who wanted change started a revolution to overthrow Díaz. This Mexican Revolution lasted for ten years, led by people such as Pancho Villa and Emiliano Zapata, who were the peasants' heroes. By the time the fighting was over, more than one million people had died. Frida grew up very aware of the struggles between the rich and the poor, and the tense situation influenced her political ideas.

> Frida's birth certificate gives her birth year as 1907, but she told everyone that she was born in 1910. She wasn't pretending to be younger. The Mexican Revolution began in 1910, and Frida changed her birth year to honor the Mexican people's gaining power and independence from the government.

When she was six, Frida developed a disease called polio. It affects the nervous system and can leave a person paralyzed. For nine months, Frida suffered from horrible pains in her legs. She couldn't walk and had to stay in bed all day. To pass the long hours, Frida created her own world. She would fog up her bedroom window with her breath and draw a door in the fog. Then, she pretended to pass through that door to play with imaginary friends.

The polio left Frida with one leg much weaker than the other. To build up strength, Frida became involved in all kinds of sports. At the time, girls were supposed to learn to cook and sew and be proper, but Guillermo knew that only exercise would help his daughter get well. He encouraged her to participate in soccer, wrestling, swimming, and even boxing.

Frida was an unusually bright child who was interested in everything around her. She wanted to become a doctor. She attended the best high school in Mexico City, the National Preparatory School. Out of the two thousand students there, only thirty-five were girls. Frida made friends quickly and started hanging out with a group that called themselves the *Cachuchas* (after the peaked hats they always wore). They had the reputation of being the smartest and most mischievous children in school. They played tricks, such as riding a donkey through the hallways or setting off firecrackers in the classes they found boring.

When Frida was about sixteen, the famous Mexican artist Diego Rivera came to her school to paint a large mural. All the students were intrigued by him. People said that Diego was a strange character who was obsessed with his art, and that he had affairs with many different women. The students weren't allowed to watch Diego paint, but Frida snuck into the auditorium where he worked and watched anyway. She would call to him in a teasing way and sometimes take food out of his lunch pail. Diego liked the spunky young student, but thought of her as just a child.

Frida dreamed of traveling through the United States and was trying to save money for the trip by working in factories or local stores. But on September 17, 1925, when she was just eighteen, her whole life changed. Frida was riding a bus with her boyfriend when a streetcar smashed into the bus. Many of the passengers were killed. At first, Frida thought she was okay, but she was actually in shock. A metal bar had gone through her body; she had a broken pelvis, leg, collarbone, and ribs; her foot was crushed; and her spine was broken in three places. An ambulance rushed her to the hospital. The doctors were sure she would die.

But Frida was a fighter. Although she was encased in a plaster bodycast and couldn't move at all, she tried to keep her spirits up and looked forward to daily visits from her sister Matilde. After a month in the hospital, Frida was sent home to complete her recovery.

Frida Kahlo and Diego Rivera

All day long, she lay on her back and tried to endure the pain she felt in every limb. She was reminded of her childhood polio and the loneliness she had felt then. By the next summer, Frida began to paint as a way of expressing her feelings. Her mother arranged for an easel to be mounted right onto Frida's bed, so she could paint lying down. She created the first of many self-portraits and sent it to her boyfriend as a gift. But their relationship didn't survive the accident.

Frida was known for her thick, dark eyebrows, which she often exaggerated in paintings. Her husband, Diego Rivera, thought they made her look like a strong woman, and described them as "the wings of a blackbird."

It took more than two years for Frida to start living normally again, though she would be in pain for the rest of her life. She started going out again and made a new group of friends who were very political. They were active Communists who believed that Mexico's poor people were being kept down by the rich, and that all citizens should share the country's wealth equally. Frida joined the Communist Party and went to rallies and group discussions. Diego Rivera was also a Communist, and Frida sometimes ran into him at the meetings. One day, she got up the courage to show him her paintings. She told him that she needed an honest opinion. If he thought that she would never make it as an artist, she wanted to know, so she could move on and do something else with her life. Diego was surprised by Frida's talent, and told her that she had to keep painting.

Frida and Diego started spending a lot of time together and grew to be close friends. Soon, to everyone's surprise, they fell in love. Most people thought they made a very odd couple. Besides the twenty-one-year age difference and the fact that Diego had already been married three times before, they looked like opposites: She was tiny and weighed just 98 pounds (45 kg); he was tall and weighed over 300 pounds (135 kg). But they also had a lot in common. Both of them had never-ending energy, enormous talent, and great passions for art and politics. It was not long before they decided to get married. Frida's parents disapproved of the match at first, but in the end they thought the marriage might be a good idea. Frida's medical bills were becoming too expensive for them, and Diego

Frida and Diego, seen here ca. 1933, were an odd-looking couple. She was tiny. He was large.

had enough money to care for her. Frida and Diego married on August 21, 1929.

Frida in 1932

The marriage changed Frida's life. She resigned from the Communist Party because they expelled Diego for doing work for the anti-Communist Mexican government. And in the fall of 1930, she and her husband moved to San Francisco where Diego had been hired to paint a mural for the Stock Exchange. While Diego worked, Frida explored the city. She began to dress in traditional Native Mexican clothing — colorful long peasant skirts and puffy blouses. She braided her hair and decorated it with flowers, combs, and ribbons. You couldn't help but notice Frida, the living work of art, as she walked down the street.

In 1932, Diego and Frida moved to Detroit, where Diego would paint another mural, this time about the city's booming car industry. Frida had mixed feelings about the United States. Her adventurous side loved exploring new places and meeting new people, but in her heart she was homesick for Mexico and missed its rich culture. She created a painting called *Self-Portrait on the Borderline Between Mexico and the United States* to express her feelings. In the painting, Frida stands between the two countries: on the American side are skyscrapers and pollution; on the Mexican side are ancient ruins and flowers.

The next year, Frida and Diego moved to New York City, where Diego was to paint a mural in Rockefeller Center. John

Some art critics tried to classify Frida's work with the work of the surrealists, whose paintings were based on their dreams. But Frida refused the label. She said, "I never painted my dreams. I painted my own reality."

D. Rockefeller, the famous and wealthy businessman, was paying for the project. Before the mural was even finished, huge controversy arose. In the painting, Diego included a figure of Vladimir Lenin, the Russian Communist leader, whom American businessmen despised. Diego refused to change his work, and so the Rockefellers fired him, paid his fee, and destroyed the mural. Frida expressed her sadness and disappointment in the visit to New York in her painting *My Dress Hangs There*. It shows New York City as a very dark and scary place, with a traditional Mexican peasant dress hanging in the middle of the picture. The dress likely represented Frida to show that while part of her was in New York, her spirit was home in Mexico.

Meanwhile, Frida and Diego's marriage, which was always full of drama and passion, was going through an especially difficult phase. Both were upset about the destruction of Diego's work in New York, but he didn't want to leave the U.S. as much as Frida did. They fought often, and Diego had a love affair with Frida's younger sister, Cristina. Frida also had love affairs with both men and women.

In December of 1933, Frida and Diego returned to Mexico City. They moved into separate houses that were connected by a bridge, so they could still live together but have a lot of privacy and time to work. Frida took advantage of the time, because she was gradually gaining respect as a talented artist, separate from her famous husband. She sometimes had difficulty working, though, because she lived in constant pain from her old injuries.

In 1938, Frida's paintings were displayed in an exhibition at the Julien Levy Gallery in New York City. The show was considered a great success and created a huge buzz in the art world. Frida rarely painted objects as they appear in real life. Her work was full of symbolism, where the objects or people represent the artist's feelings and views. Frida often painted monkeys, and many believe that the monkeys symbolized the children that Frida never had.

One of the biggest admirers of Frida's work was the French Surrealist painter

Frida with *Self Portrait as a Tehuana*, painted in 1943

André Breton. He invited her to Paris to take part in an exhibition he organized called *Mexique*. It was Frida's first visit to Europe and the adventure was thrilling. She didn't sell many paintings, because World War II was about to break out and no one had money to buy art, but it was a great experience that spread the word about the talented Mexican artist.

In 1939, Frida and Diego decided to end their troubled

Frida in her studio with *The Two Fridas*, Coyoacán, Mexico, ca. 1943

relationship and divorced. Losing her best friend and husband left Frida heartbroken and once again she turned to painting for comfort and to work out her feelings. In one of her most famous works, *The Two Fridas*, she painted two self-portraits. One Frida is the person that Diego loved, and the other is the person that Diego left. She painted the Fridas' hearts on the outside of their bodies. Despite the deep heartbreak Frida expressed in this painting, the bond she shared with Diego was too strong to be broken — they married each other again in December of 1940.

In 1943, Frida took on the role of teacher at a new art school in Mexico City, La Esmeralda, that offered classes for free. Frida taught many students who came from poor families and could not afford to pay for art classes. She enjoyed spending time with her students and seeing their work progress, but health problems sometimes kept her from her job. On those days, she held classes in her own home and took turns resting and helping the students with their work.

Three years later, Frida went to New York City to have an operation on her spine. Over the years, she'd gone through many treatments in hopes that she could live pain-free — she'd worn twenty-eight different types of corsets to support her back, she'd hung by her hands from metal rings, and she'd even spent twelve weeks sitting perfectly straight with sandbags on her feet — but nothing seemed to help. At first, she felt better after the operation in New York, but the relief didn't last long. Once she returned to Mexico to recover, she was lucky to have a lot of friends visit her. She also felt comforted by the many animals she kept as pets — monkeys, birds, a deer, and even an eagle.

By April of 1953, Frida's body was so worn out that she could not leave her bed, even though she wanted to do so more than anything. Her first solo exhibition in Mexico City was opening at the Galeria Arte Contemporaneo, and she wanted desperately to be there. But her doctors insisted that she stay in bed. As ill as she was, Frida insisted on attending her own exhibition. An ambulance took her to the gallery, where a big four-poster bed was set up. Frida spent the evening in that bed, celebrating with her friends and fans. The opening was a great success.

Despite her positive attitude, Frida's health continued to get worse. In August of the same year, her right leg was amputated at the knee, and she had to wear an artificial leg. Still, she continued to paint whenever she had the strength, usually lying in bed or sitting in a wheelchair.

On July 13, 1954, Frida died. She was only forty-seven years old. As her coffin was carried through the streets of Mexico City to the cemetery, five hundred mourners walked behind it. Her death nearly destroyed Diego. He said that although not everyone recognized it, Frida Kahlo was a much better painter than he ever was. Three years later, Diego died at the age of seventy.

Today, Frida's work is more popular than ever, as more people appreciate her creativity, her originality, and learn the story of how she struggled for her art. The blue house where she grew up has been kept as a museum, and thousands of people come to visit it every year to see where Frida worked and got her inspiration. She is one of the country's best-loved artists. Mexicans refer to Frida as "the soul of Mexico."

> You can see some of Frida's paintings on the Internet at the website for the American Public Broadcasting Service (PBS). **www.pbs.org/weta/fridakahlo/resources/locations.html**

ELIZABETH CATLETT

1915 -

ART IS FOR EVERYONE

We all have struggles in our lives, but Elizabeth Catlett has faced more than her fair share throughout her long career. Determined to become a great artist, Elizabeth experienced racism, sexism, and even political difficulties. But she never gave up. Her own experiences and seeing how some people, such as the poor or people of color, were excluded from the art world inspired Elizabeth's dream to bring art to them. She followed her passion and painted the lives of women who didn't have a strong voice in society. She made art for people of all colors, classes, and genders to enjoy.

Alice Elizabeth Catlett was born on April 15, 1915, in Washington, DC. Her father, John Catlett, was a math teacher who had an artistic side. His hobbies were playing music and woodcarving. John died just a few months before little Elizabeth's birth, but she may have inherited his artistic talents. Elizabeth's mother, Mary Carson Catlett, was also trained as a teacher. After her husband's death, she worked long hours as a cleaning woman to support her three children. Neighbors cared for baby Elizabeth during the day.

Mary encouraged her daughter's talent for drawing, which was obvious from the time she first learned to hold a crayon. Mary brought home pens and colored pencils and paper — anything Elizabeth could use for making pictures.

Elizabeth grew up in a family that believed in education and hard work — not just because both of her parents were teachers, or because Mary had to work hard to support the family, but also because Elizabeth's ancestors had struggled a lot. They hoped that future generations would have better lives. Her great-grandmother had been kidnapped from Madagascar and brought to America to work as a slave. Three of Elizabeth's grandparents were slaves in the southern United States. They were forced to work long hours without pay for the slave owners. Mary made sure that her children knew their heritage and reminded them that as African Americans, they should honor the family's struggles, be proud, and always work hard. Elizabeth knew that as a woman of color, she might face racism some day, and that she would have to be brave and rise above it.

Elizabeth started kindergarten at Lucretia Mott Elementary School. She was used to being away from home all day at the babysitter's, so she wasn't nervous about beginning school. By the time she was about nine years old, she was in the advanced class that studied French and algebra. Besides being a smart girl, what set Elizabeth apart from other children was her artistic flair. Teachers and students all admired her drawings, paintings, and small sculptures made of soap. By the time she graduated with honors from Dunbar High School, Elizabeth had serious dreams of becom-

> "I think people should create art because they want to create...I don't think they should create to make money. I don't think they should create to be important, to be famous."
>
> —Elizabeth Catlett

ing a painter some day. She didn't know of any other female African American artists, but she knew she could achieve her dream, even without role models.

Because she loved school and believed that continuing her education would make her a great artist, Elizabeth applied to the art department of the Carnegie Institute of Technology in Pittsburg. But not everyone thought this school should be her first choice. Applying to Carnegie was pointless, her family said, because Carnegie only admitted white students. Elizabeth ignored the warnings and applied anyway. Carnegie's entrance exams lasted a whole week, and Elizabeth worked very hard to show her talent and her knowledge of art. She overheard the teachers talking about her, praising her work. She was happy until she heard one teacher say, "It's too bad she's colored."

Despite the racist comment, Elizabeth believed she had a chance of getting accepted into the school. When the letter came telling her that she had not been chosen to study at Carnegie, Elizabeth was deeply disappointed.

Rather than give up, Elizabeth picked up the pieces of her dream and kept going. She applied and was accepted at the Howard University School of Fine Arts, where she majored in painting. There, Elizabeth learned about printmaking (using a printing plate or stamp to create many copies of a work) and drawing techniques. She studied under famous Black artists such as Lois Mailou Jones, James Wells, and James Porter.

Professor Porter became her mentor. He believed in her potential, let her use his personal library, and talked with her about art. In 1935, Elizabeth graduated with high honors.

Even though she did really well at Howard University, the rejection from Carnegie haunted Elizabeth. Not because she didn't get into the school, but because she was rejected for being Black. She remembered the stories of how her grandparents had struggled as slaves; and she thought about how some museums in the southern United States refused to exhibit any works by Black artists. Elizabeth knew she couldn't sit back and allow these injustices to go on.

In 1937, Elizabeth took a job as an art teacher in elementary schools in Durham, North Carolina. Schools in that state and many others were segregated at the time, meaning that Black students and white students were separated and not allowed to attend the same schools. Through talking with other teachers and principals, Elizabeth learned that white teachers' salaries were a lot higher than those of Black teachers, and she started a campaign for equal pay for all teachers. The campaign didn't succeed, but Elizabeth still believed that speaking up for equal rights was always worthwhile.

Although Elizabeth enjoyed teaching, she felt it took up far too much of her time. After all, she wanted to be an artist, not a teacher. She enrolled in the State University of Iowa (now University of Iowa) to get her Masters of Fine Arts degree. Elizabeth was one of only two Black students in the art department. Even though she was allowed to attend the school, Elizabeth was not allowed to stay in the dorm with white students and had to find a place to live off campus.

At the university, Elizabeth found another mentor, the painter Grant Wood. He taught her that to be an artist requires a lot of discipline. Most importantly, he taught Elizabeth that the subjects of her art should be those things she knew best — that she should take inspiration from her own life.

In Elizabeth's second year of graduate studies, she changed her major to sculpture. She loved working with the solid materials and carving tools to create art from terra cotta (clay), wood, plaster, and bronze. For her final exam piece, she created a limestone statue of a mother holding her baby, called *Negro Mother and Child*. (Elizabeth's favorite subjects throughout her career would be Black women and the relationship between mothers and their children.) At the time, not many artists showed the real lives of Black women, and Elizabeth wanted her art to give those women a voice. She used her work to express herself and to show that art is for everyone, regardless of race or gender. Elizabeth also exhibited sculptures at the school's gallery and became the first person to earn a Master of Fine Arts degree in sculpture at the State University of Iowa, in 1940.

After graduation, Elizabeth accepted a job as the chair of the art department at Dillard University in New Orleans. She worked there for two years and faced many challenges in that short time. Elizabeth had her students paint and draw live nude models, which some people found quite scandalous. She also dealt with segregation and racism in the city. Every day as she rode the bus to work, she was forced to sit in the back. The buses were segregated, so only white people could sit in the front. Signs saying "For colored only" were posted by the back seats. Elizabeth ripped those signs down when the driver wasn't looking.

When Elizabeth heard that an exhibition of the famous Spanish painter Pablo Picasso was coming to New Orleans, she couldn't wait to bring her students. But a problem arose. The exhibition was at the Delgado Museum (which is now called the New Orleans Museum of Art). The Delgado was located in the middle of a park that Black people were not allowed to enter. To get around the rule, Elizabeth had buses drop off all of her 160 students right at the front door of the museum.

Elizabeth married a fellow artist, Charles White, in 1942. She met him in Chicago, where she was taking a summer course in ceramics at the The Art Institute of Chicago. The couple moved to Harlem, New York. The city buzzed with the energy of great artists and thinkers who lived there at the time, such as the poet Langston Hughes and the painter and muralist Aaron Douglas.

New ideas about art were all around her, and Elizabeth took private lessons with the Russian sculptor Ossip Zadkine

Elizabeth Catlett with one of her striking works

and studied at the Art Students League in 1944. Then she took a teaching job at George Washington Carver School, where she taught sculpture and even dressmaking to working-class people, mostly of African American and Latino descent.

> "I have gradually reached the conclusion that art is important only to the extent that it aids in the liberation of our people."
> —Elizabeth Catlett

The school was designed to give poor people access to the kinds of education and culture that they didn't have normally. Most of the students worked long hours at their day jobs, so they took night classes.

Despite Elizabeth's hard work, she still felt frustrated at times. Other artists thought of her as Charles's wife, or the wife of an artist, instead of an artist in her own right. Elizabeth was determined to change these attitudes.

In 1945, she applied for the Rosenwald Fellowship, a scholarship that would help her continue studying and working on her art. She proposed to create a series of prints, paintings, and sculptures about the lives of African American women. When she was awarded the fellowship, Elizabeth moved to Mexico in 1946. She knew that in Mexico, artists such as Diego Rivera painted murals in public spaces, making art for all people to see. And because Elizabeth strongly believed that art should be accessible to everyone, she believed Mexico would be inspiring. Elizabeth thought she would stay for perhaps a year or so and had little idea of how much living in Mexico would change her life.

That year Elizabeth joined an artists' group in Mexico City called Taller de Gráfica Popular (People's Graphic Arts Workshop). She shared workspace and materials with thirty other Mexican artists and activists. They created inexpensive prints so that poor people could buy and enjoy art. Elizabeth also combined her love of art with her love of social activism. She campaigned for the rights of students and unions, promoted adult literacy, and created posters, flyers, and illustrations for books.

Although Elizabeth's work life was going well, her marriage was not. Elizabeth saw her own life heading in a direction that was much different from the life she and Charles shared. After she and her husband divorced, Elizabeth met someone who was a much better match for her. Francisco Mora, a Mexican painter and printmaker, married Elizabeth in 1947, and she decided to make Mexico her permanent home.

Working at the Taller was very productive for Elizabeth. She created many works that showed the lives and struggles of Black women in a powerful way. The paintings, that together were called the *Negro Woman* series, showed strong images of African American women. Sometimes they were doing regular activities such as working or reading, but the women always looked proud. Elizabeth also created a series of paintings about Harriet Tubman, a heroic Black woman who helped slaves escape through the Underground Railroad, which was a series of secret passages and safe houses that slaves used to make their way to freedom in Canada. Elizabeth was also inspired by the lives of the Mexican people among whom she lived, and they became important subjects in her art as well.

Elizabeth had to juggle her artistic life and her home life carefully. Between 1947 and 1951, she and Francisco had three sons (David, Francisco, and Juan) who were all smart children with artistic talents. The first became an artist, the second a jazz musician, and the third a filmmaker.

> "Art can't be the exclusive domain of the [elite]. It belongs to everyone. Artists should work to the end that love, peace, justice and equal opportunity prevail all over the world."
>
> —Elizabeth Catlett

In 1955, Elizabeth returned to sculpture. Though she could only sculpt in the mornings when her sons were at school, she threw herself back into the work. In 1959, when her children were a bit older, she took a job teaching sculpture at Universidad Nacional Autónoma de México. She was the first woman ever to teach at the University. Some male teachers and students were against having a female teacher on the faculty, but Elizabeth did such a great job that she was promoted to be the director of the sculpture department. She kept that job until 1975.

In 1962, Elizabeth had her first solo exhibition in Mexico. It featured sculptures of bronze, wood, and terra cotta, as well as some prints. Over the next several years, she won top prizes in national sculpture competitions.

In that same year, Elizabeth became a Mexican citizen, but she continued to keep up with news from the United States. In 1970, she was invited to be an Elder of Distinction at a conference on Black art at Northwestern University in Chicago. However, the United States Embassy wouldn't give her permission to travel to the U.S. At the time, the political situation in the U.S. was tense, and people such as Elizabeth who actively spoke out for equal rights and political power for citizens were considered troublemakers. For about eight years, the State Department of the United States refused to let Elizabeth cross the border.

The barrier broke in 1971, when the Studio Museum in Harlem held an exhibition of Elizabeth's work entitled *Elizabeth Catlett: Prints and Sculpture*. Many artists petitioned the State Department to give Elizabeth permission to come to the opening. Finally, she was allowed to return to the country of her birth for the exciting occasion. The show was a huge success, and for the next twenty years, Elizabeth had exhibitions in many other American galleries. In 1975, the city of New Orleans commissioned Elizabeth to create a 10-foot (3-meter) tall bronze statue of the jazz musician Louis Armstrong for display in Armstrong Park.

Another successful exhibition at the June Kelly Gallery in Manhattan in 1993 led to Elizabeth's works being sold to the Baltimore Museum of Art, New Orleans Museum of Art, and the Metropolitan Museum in New York City. The Neuberger Museum of Art in Purchase, New York, held a fifty-year retrospective (a tribute to her long career) of Elizabeth's work in 1998.

Elizabeth Catlett is still producing art and using her work to tell the stories of Black women. The idea of art for everyone continues to be very important to her, and she believes that art in public spaces can make the world a more beautiful and interesting place for people of all backgrounds, social positions, and genders. In 2002, the U.S. Embassy in Mexico granted her dual citizenship, so she now divides her time between Cuernavaca, Mexico, and New York.

> Many museums have Elizabeth Catlett's work as part of their permanent collections. Visit the National Museum of Women in the Arts (**www.nmwa.org**), the Lauren Rogers Museum of Art (**www.lrma.org**), and the Muskegon Museum of Art (**www. muskegonartmuseum.org**) to see some of Elizabeth's work.

KENOJUAK ASHEVAK

1927 -

INUIT LIFE AND ART

The act of creating art is very powerful. Through the joy, inspiration, and independent thinking that it brings, creating art can even help an artist survive difficult times in her life. The Inuit artist Kenojuak Ashevak has coped with a lot of change and hardship in her life. But thanks to her art that draws on her cultural heritage, she has been able to stay focused, positive, successful.

The Inuit are some of Canada's First Peoples. They live far north, in the Arctic. They had little contact with white explorers until the 1950s (when the Canadian government started

81

programs to encourage the Inuit to abandon their traditional ways), because visitors couldn't live in the harsh conditions. To survive the long, dark winters and temperatures of -40° F (-40° C) or lower, the Inuit relied on their great knowledge of nature and their sharp hunting skills. They hunted animals such as seals, whales, and caribou, and used all of what they caught: meat for eating; animals skins to make clothing, boats, and tents; bones to make tools; and sinew to make thread. The Inuit didn't own land, because they believed that land belongs to everyone. They lived in small groups and moved with the seasons, followed the patterns of migrating animals.

Kenojuak's family lived according to the traditional Inuit ways. She was born in an igloo on the southwest coast of Baffin Island, Nunavut. Today, much of the island's population lives in Iqaluit, Nunavut's capital. Her birth date was around October 3, 1927, but the exact date was never documented. Kenojuak was named after her dead grandfather on her mother's side. The Inuit believe that naming a child after someone who has passed away gives the child all the love and respect that the dead person once had. Kenojuak's father, Ushuaqjuk, was the son of a shaman (*angakkuq*), which is someone who is thought to have great powers for healing others and predicting the future. Many people believed that Ushuaqjuk had these powers, too.

As a young girl, Kenojuak felt very close to her father. She admired him because he was a kind person who often shared his family's food with others who had none. He was also an excellent hunter. But he sometimes got into arguments because he liked to be independent and didn't always follow the rules of the camp. On one bitterly cold winter day, when Kenojuak was only six years old, Ushuaqjuk's independence would cost him dearly — he was shot and murdered by three men after an argument. The Inuit had no court or jail system, and the men were never punished.

At the time of her husband's death, Kenojuak's mother, Silaqqi, was pregnant with her fourth child. She knew she needed to rejoin her family and escape the bad memories of her husband's death. And so, Kenojuak's family traveled to Cape Dorset aboard a ship called the *Nascopie*. Run by the Hudson's Bay Company, the ship brought supplies to the Inuit people once a year because there were no stores up north that sold the things they needed. When they arrived at their destination, Camp Sapujjuaq, Kenojuak stayed with her grandmother, Quitsaq.

Kenojuak Ashevak's art is exhibited in many major collections, such as the Canadian Museum of Civilization, the McMichael Canadian Art Collection, the Montreal Museum of Fine Arts, the National Gallery of Canada, the Royal Ontario Museum, and the Vancouver Art Gallery.

The next few years were very happy ones. Kenojuak spent most of her time fishing, hunting, and tracking birds and small animals. She loved to observe wildlife, especially birds, and admired the beautiful way they moved. Kenojuak grew very close to her grandmother, who taught her granddaughter many important skills. By the time Kenojuak was about eight years old, she knew how to sew using caribou sinew to make watertight stitching. She helped out by fixing small rips in skins that were to be traded with the Hudson's Bay Company. And best of all, she was allowed to make sealskin bags and decorate them with her own designs.

Kenojuak didn't always stay in Cape Dorset. Her family had to follow migrating animals, because hunting was their main source of food. Sometimes she traveled with her mother and stepfather, or with her uncles to other camps. When it was very cold out, Kenojuak stayed in an igloo or a *qarmaq* (a house made of moss) and when it was warm she slept in a *haumuq* (tent).

By the time she was about nineteen, Kenojuak knew she would be getting married soon. In fact, many girls she knew had gotten married even younger. Inuit marriages helped join families together, and formed a partnership between the man and the woman so they could take care of each other. Young people couldn't always choose their partners, and Kenojuak was nervous. She was happy with her life as it was. If she married, everything would change.

Around 1946, visitors came to speak with Silaqqi. Kenojuak pretended to be asleep in her tent, but really she was listening to the visitors talk. Their brother, Jonniebo, had sent them to ask Kenojuak's relatives if he could become her husband. Everyone agreed that it would be a good match. Although she had met him a few times before, all Kenojuak knew of Jonniebo was that he was tall and he smiled a lot.

That summer, the *Nascopie* came to Cape Dorset bearing supplies as it did every year. When the ship left, Kenojuak also left with Jonniebo. They were married, but according to Inuit custom, they didn't need a fancy ceremony to cement their union. At first, Kenojuak made it very clear that she wasn't thrilled about being Jonniebo's wife. Sometimes, she even threw pebbles at him when he came near. But he understood that she was nervous being away from her family, and gave her time to get used to her new life. When she was certain that Jonniebo was a kind and loyal man, Kenojuak grew to love him.

The young couple lived in a few different camps together, but didn't have a permanent home. In the fall of 1946, they moved to a camp at Keakto near Cape Dorset. It was close to the open sea, which made it a good spot for hunting. That winter, they lived in an igloo. At Keakto, as in other Inuit camps, the men worked together, hunting and ensuring that there was enough food for everyone. The women made sure everything at the camp ran smoothly. Besides caring for children and preparing meals, they prepared animal skins, stretching the hides and scraping them until they were clean. Performing these duties requires lots of skill, but Kenojuak never felt that she truly mastered them, as other women did.

A year after being married, Kenojuak had her first child, a boy named Jamasie. In Inuit culture, women band together to help the mother through labor, and Kenojuak had four midwives in her tent. After the birth, Kenojuak had to get right back to work. She continued her daily duties and carried Jamasie around in her *amautik* (a warm hooded parka). Her second child, a girl named Mary, was born in 1949.

Big changes started happening in the Inuit communities around 1950. More and more, white people came and tried to force their ways on the Inuit. The Baffin Island Trading Company on Cape Dorset closed, and many people had little money or supplies. The Canadian government set up many Inuit in permanent homes and gave them some money, but times were still difficult, and the change forced the Inuit to abandon many of their traditional ways. The Royal Canadian Mounted Police began to record births, deaths, and marriages among Inuit people and gave every person a number according to where they were from. Kenojuak was E7-1035. A nurse and a teacher came to Cape Dorset and children attended school. They weren't taught about their heritage; they were forced to learn white, European ways. And although they were already married, an Anglican missionary came and married Kenojuak and Jonniebo in a Christian ceremony.

In 1951, government medical workers told Kenojuak that she had tuberculosis, a contagious lung disease. They told her that she had to stay in a hospital until she got better. That meant leaving her children and husband behind, and going to a strange place. But Kenojuak had no choice. Just before she left, she gave birth to a baby boy. Because she wouldn't be there to care for him, her cousins adopted the child. In Inuit

Kenojuak Ashevak with her work in Cape Dorset, Nunavut, 1980

culture, children are a responsibility of the community, and for children to be adopted by family members or close friends is very common.

Although she was frightened, Kenojuak tried to be brave. She and a few others took their first-ever airplane ride to a hospital in Quebec City in 1952. Many other Inuit people were being treated for tuberculosis. Some got better, and some died. The patients kept each other company, but the days passed very slowly for Kenojuak. She missed Cape Dorset desperately and couldn't wait to return. Kenojuak was so ill that she almost died twice, but she thought of her family and tried to stay strong. As her health improved, Kenojuak kept busy by sewing and doing beadwork and leatherwork. An art teacher at the hospital sold her creations and gave her the money from the sales.

After three and a half years away, Kenojuak boarded a ship back to Cape Dorset. But she had some difficulties getting settled into her old life. Kenojuak found that she had lost many of her skills because she hadn't practiced them; she had even completely forgotten how to sew with caribou sinew, something she learned as a little girl. Also, the fur trade was no longer a good income for the Inuit, and people were poor and had little food.

To make money, Kenojuak participated in an Inuit art program led by a government worker and artist, James Houston, and his wife, Alma. The Inuit called James *Saumik* ("Left-handed one") and Alma, *Arnakotak* ("Tall lady"). The Houstons believed that by creating and selling Inuit art, the people, especially women, would gain some independence and be able to help their

In Inuktitut, the language of the Inuit people, there is no word for "art." Instead, they use the word *sananquaq*, which means "making a likeness." To them, art is turning something real into something unreal.

You may notice that the signature on Kenojuak's prints is very unique. First is the symbol for Kenojuak's name. Beneath it is the stone carver's symbol. And last is a tiny red or black symbol that looks like an upside-down "U." It represents an igloo, and it is the symbol for artists from the Cape Dorset community.

families. James and Alma were also amazed at the beauty of Inuit carvings and drawings and wanted to share them with the world. Kenojuak made and decorated tiny wooden carvings and sealskin bags, which were sold through the Hudson's Bay Company. The Houstons knew that her work was special and encouraged her to be creative and make whatever she wished. Kenojuak never thought of herself as an artist, but she soon uncovered her hidden talents.

In 1958, Kenojuak made her first print, called *Rabbit Eating Seaweed*. It appeared as a design on a sealskin bag. There are many ways to make a print, and Kenojuak's print was made in a way that required many people working together to reproduce her drawing. First, an artist draws an image. Next, a carver chisels the image onto a stone block. Then, paint is applied to the stone block with a roller. While the paint is still wet, a thin sheet of paper is pressed onto the block, and the image is transferred to the paper. Usually, only a limited number of copies of one image are made (perhaps fifty), to preserve its uniqueness. Kenojuak also began to make drawings on paper using colored pencils. At first, she didn't know what to draw. She even tore up her first drawing. But as she gained confidence, she found inspiration in her own life.

Stories, legends, and dreams are often the subjects of Inuit art. Inuit people relied on storytelling and artwork to pass down their history. But Kenojuak's art is a bit different, because she prefers to draw from her everyday reality, from what she sees in life rather than what she hears in stories. One of Kenojuak's favorite subjects is animals — polar bears,

Kenojuak Ashevak takes a break from drawing in
Cape Dorset, Nunavut, 1997.

fish, dogs, and especially birds. She draws them in a bold style, using strong lines, to show their strength. One of her best-known works, *The Enchanted Owl*, was honored on a Canadian stamp in 1970. She does not always know why or how she chooses her subjects, they simply come to her as she draws. Jonniebo once said that perhaps Kenojuak's artistic ideas come from spirits whispering in her ear.

By the 1960s, Kenojuak was becoming well-known throughout Canada as a great artist. She began to experiment with copper engravings, with beautiful results. She was even the subject of a film called *Eskimo Artist — Kenojuak*, which was filmed on Cape Dorset. She found movie-making tiresome, but the money she earned paid for a new kayak for Jonniebo.

The success she experienced grew to greater heights. In 1967, Kenojuak traveled to Ottawa to receive the Order of Canada for her excellent contribution to art in the Inuit community. The National Library of Canada held an exhibition for

The Enchanted Owl on Canadian stamps

the occasion, which featured forty-five works by Kenojuak and five by Jonniebo. Three years later, she returned to Ottawa for a very special project. She and Jonniebo worked together on a 23-by-26-foot (7-by-8-meter) mural for the Canadian pavilion at Expo 1970, which was to be held in Osaka, Japan. For three months, Kenojuak, Jonniebo, and their three children, Adamie, Pee, and Pudlo, lived in an apartment in the city, which was quite an adventure for them. Later on, Kenojuak traveled to Japan and felt so proud to see her work displayed so far from home.

The same year, Kenojuak and her husband chose their last name, Ashevak (after Jonniebo's father), because the Canadian government had stopped identifying the Inuit by numbers.

The joy Kenojuak found in creating her art helped her deal with many personal tragedies. Because of tuberculosis and poor medical care, not all Inuit children grew up to become adults. Kenojuak's first three children passed away when they were quite young, and she later gave birth to other children, some of whom didn't live more than a few months. Sadly, Jonniebo's health was also poor and not getting better. He died in 1972. Over the next ten years, Kenojuak had two other partners, but both of them died as well. But she kept up her art, not only because she loved it, but also because she had children to support. Her whirlwind career continued. In 1980, she made the long journey to the Netherlands for the opening of the "Inuit Print" exhibition.

At home, Kenojuak has received many honors as one of the most important Inuit artists. Her print *The Return of the Sun*, which she made in 1961, was used on Canada Post's 17-cent stamp. She was awarded one of Canada's highest honors two years later, when she was made a Companion of the Order of Canada for her lifetime of outstanding achievement in art. Kenojuak even has two honorary doctorates: one from Queen's University and the other from the University of Toronto.

In 1995, Kenojuak received the National Aboriginal Achievement Award for a lifetime of creativity. And when Nunavut became its own official territory on April 1, 1999, the Canadian Mint issued a special coin bearing Kenojuak's design of an owl. She also became the very first Inuit artist to be inducted into Canada's Walk of Fame in 2001.

Kenojuak Ashevak still lives in Cape Dorset and she loves to spend time with her many grandchildren. A woman in her eighties, she continues to draw and is known internationally as one of Canada's leading female artists. Through her art, she not only found a career, but also shared the rich Inuit culture with the rest of the world. In Kenojuak's own words: "I cannot imagine life without art."

> You can see some of Kenojuak Ashevak's art online at the website of the Houston North Gallery.
> **www.houston-north-gallery.ns.ca/Kenojuak.html**

FAITH RINGGOLD

1930 -

TELLING STORIES THROUGH ART

Art can express very personal feelings, such as how an artist feels about her family and her own identity. Art can also make strong statements that show the artist's point of view on public issues, such as racism, sexism, and politics. Faith Ringgold's art does both of these things. She fearlessly lets her art show who she is — an African American woman — and what she thinks about the world around her.

On October 8, 1930, Willi Posey Jones and Andrew Louis Jones had a baby girl at Harlem Hospital in New York City. Even though they were happy to have a new baby in the family,

Willi and Andrew couldn't help but feel sad at first. Their 18-month-old son had just died of pneumonia. The couple was still grieving and had been hoping to have another baby boy. The nurse at the hospital sensed their sadness and suggested that they name their new daughter Faith, to remind them to believe in a better tomorrow. The Joneses took her message to heart and called their baby girl Faith Willi Jones.

The whole family adored Faith. Her brother, Andrew Jr., and sister, Barb, would wrap her in colorful quilts to keep her snug and take her for long walks in a baby buggy down 146th Street. They were thrilled to have a little sister.

Faith was a delicate baby who needed special care. She had trouble with her breathing because she got asthma when she was two. Because of her condition, Faith couldn't go to kindergarten or grade one. Willi didn't want to take any chances with her daughter's health. She was worried that Faith might catch polio, a disease of the nervous system, or tuberculosis, a lung disease, if she went to school while she was still weak. Little Faith was given only healthy foods, such as vegetables, fruits, fresh meat, cornmeal gruel, and wholesome homemade cookies. Sometimes she complained because she couldn't have candy like her brother and sister, but she tried to follow the special diet.

The Great Depression, which took place during the 1930s, was a terribly difficult time. Jobs were very hard to find and many people were homeless. Luckily, Andrew had a good job working for the city's Department of Sanitation, and he earned a very good wage for the time — about $34 per week. So while the Joneses weren't rich, they had enough money to support the children and put food on the table.

For the first few years of her life, Faith spent a lot of time at home. Willi bought textbooks and taught her daughter at home because she was still too weak to go to school. Sometimes, on special days, she took Faith to museums to

show her great works of art, or to con-
certs at the Apollo Theater and the
Paramount Theater, where legendary
entertainers such as Billie Holiday,
Lena Horne, Count Basie, and Ella
Fitzgerald performed. Faith loved seeing how they expressed themselves
through their art and wondered if she
could do the same thing some day.

> Faith holds sixteen honorary degrees from universities all over the United States, such as the California College of Arts and Crafts, the Rhode Island School of Design, Chicago Institute of the Arts, and the City College of New York.

Besides learning from books and
field trips, Faith learned by creating.
Willi was a skilled and creative seamstress, so she encouraged Faith to
work with her hands. The young girl drew pictures with cray-
ons and learned how to sew. Using scraps of material, a needle,
and thread, Faith made purses and hats that she designed
herself.

Willi and Andrew divorced when Faith was twelve. She
lived with her mother and siblings, but saw her father often. By
this time, Faith was well enough to attend school regularly and
was already thinking about her future. Women didn't have as
many choices then as they do today, and people often assumed
that girls would get married and have children, not work outside the home. But Faith's mom was a great role model. She
had a career as a fashion designer and seamstress. Willi told
all three of her children that they would definitely attend college when they were old enough. She encouraged them all to
do something useful with their lives.

Young Faith knew that she wanted to be an artist and
hoped to study art at the City College of New York. She took
art classes at her elementary school and practiced drawing at
home. She made her family members pose for portraits, even
though they sometimes grew restless from having to sit still
for too long.

In 1948, Faith graduated from high school and applied to the City College as she had planned. There was just one problem — only boys could attend the school of arts. But Faith had an idea. She applied to the school of education, which did admit women. That way she could study art and earn a degree to become a teacher.

Although Faith enjoyed her classes, her time at City College certainly wasn't easy. She even had one professor who told her that her drawings weren't good enough, and that she would never become an artist. She also became frustrated with the way she was learning about art. Most of the classes focused on white, European artists and their techniques. She was assigned to draw busts (statues of a head and shoulders) of Greek figures and copy works of master painters such as Rembrandt and Cézanne. This didn't really interest Faith. As an African American woman, she wanted to create art about her own culture and history. She taught herself to mix paints to make Black skin-tones and thought about how she could use her own experiences in her work.

Besides her working life, Faith's personal life was very busy as well. By 1952, she'd married Robert Earl Wallace, a classical and jazz pianist, and had two daughters, Michele and Barbara. At first, Faith was sure that she and Earl were meant for each other. She had high hopes for their future together, she as an artist and he as a musician. But the couple soon found out how difficult life can be for young people just start-ing out, and they began to argue often. Faith had set high goals for herself, and she didn't feel that Earl shared or understood her ambition. They were separated by 1954, but Faith focused on her work and managed to finish her fine arts degree and get her teacher's license by 1955.

Faith then began what would become an eighteen-year career as an art teacher in the public school system. She loved seeing her students take interest in art and found inspiration in their creativity. During the summer breaks, Faith spent her time in Provincetown, Massachusetts, where she produced oil paintings of ocean scenes and houses. She still hadn't discovered the bold, original direction that her art would take.

While teaching, Faith kept up with her own education. In 1959, she earned her Master's degree in art from the City College. Two years later, Faith, her mother, and her two daughters embarked on an adventure and traveled to France. The women visited all the great museums in Paris, Nice, Rome, and Florence. Seeing the amazing works of art gave Faith a lot of inspiration for her own work.

The trip to Europe was an unforgettable experience, but Faith was happy to return home for a couple of reasons. She felt energized and was eager to start painting again. Also, she had a special friend, Burdette (Birdie) Ringgold, whom she missed very much. From the start, Faith and Birdie respected and trusted each other, and soon they fell in love. They married on May 19, 1962, and Faith took Birdie's last name. He was very supportive of Faith's dreams of becoming a famous artist and wanted to help her career. He encouraged her to create art based on her African American heritage and to develop her own unique style. Birdie was also happy to be Michele and Barbara's stepfather and loved them as if they were his biological daughters.

Faith wanted to share her work with other people and decided to look for a gallery to show her paintings. Although she visited art dealers and galleries all over New York City, Faith could not find a place that would show her work. Many dealers simply weren't interested in women artists, particularly Black women artists, and dismissed her work. Despite the rejection, Faith found a lot of comfort in talking to successful Black artists who had overcome prejudice, such as Hale Woodruff, Lois Mailou Jones, and Romare Bearden. In 1966 the Spectrum Gallery held the first exhibition of African American artists in more than thirty years and Faith was thrilled to be included in the show. The next year, Faith had her first solo show at the same gallery.

Talking with other artists — and dealing with people who didn't think Black women could even be artists — made Faith even more passionate about equality and art. She took part in protests against galleries that refused to show women artists. She also supported the civil rights movement, which fought for the equality for people of all races in America.

Faith expressed her strong beliefs in her work. Her 1967 mural called *The Flag Is Bleeding* shows an African American man next to a white woman and a white man. Over top of them is an American flag that is splattered with red. It shows Faith's reaction to the violence and demonstrations that were going on all over the country at the time in the struggle for racial equality.

One ordinary day in 1972, the direction of Faith's work changed in a big way. As usual, she was teaching an art class. She encouraged her students to try creating art with colorful beads and different kinds of fabrics, which are traditional art materials of African women. One student looked puzzled and asked Faith why she didn't use these materials in her own work. Faith couldn't answer that question and realized then that if she used fabrics and beads for her art, she just might feel more connected with her heritage. Then, during a trip to Holland and Germany that same year to participate in a show featuring American women artists, Faith saw an exhibition of Tibetan artists who used soft cloth frames for paintings, rather than wooden ones. The frames were called *tankas*. Faith began to create colorful tankas to surround her own paintings.

Fabric became an even more important material in Faith's work when she began to create "soft" sculptures. Rather than being carved out of rock, wood, or clay, these sculptures were like large dolls dressed in real clothing, which Willi often helped to sew. In 1973 Faith created *Mrs. Jones and Family*, soft sculptures based on her own family. In 1975 she made a soft sculpture of Dr. Martin Luther King Jr., the great civil rights leader. Faith was never afraid to express herself both personally and politically in her art.

When Faith's sculptures and paintings really started to take off in 1973, she decided to stop teaching so she could focus on her art. Being able to spend as much time as she liked on her own work made her more productive than ever. She continued to experiment and push her creativity to its limits. In 1975, she put together an all African American women's art show at the Women's Interarts Center. To go along with her visual art, she also began to create performance pieces (a kind of art where the artist might use music, dance, poetry, and dialogue and perform her work for an audience in a theatrical way). One was called *The Wake and Resurrection of the Bicentennial Negro.*

The biggest goal of Faith's work was to express who she was as an African American woman, and she was always looking for unique ways to tell her story through her art. Around 1980, Faith began to create her signature style of art: quilts. Willi had told her daughter stories of their ancestors, particularly

Faith's great-great-grandmother, an African slave whose job was to make quilts for the plantation owners. The skill was passed down through the generations, and the quilts became more colorful and decorative. Quilt-making was also an opportunity for women to get together and have fun. With help from Willi, Faith began to make painted quilts, which were unlike any art most people had ever seen. Once a quilt was sewn using

> "After I decided to be an artist, the first thing that I had to believe was that I, a Black woman, could be on the art scene without sacrificing one iota of my Blackness, or my femaleness, or my humanity."
> —Faith Ringgold

> Faith's daughter Michele Wallace is an accomplished feminist scholar who published her first book when she was only twenty-seven. Michele has written books about subjects such as sexism and the identity of Black American women. She is a professor of English at City College in New York.

colored and patterned bits of fabric, Faith painted directly on top of the quilt. Faith's favorite subject was people, and she always made sure that the characters on her quilts told a story through their expressions and actions, much like a picture book.

In 1981, Willi passed away. Losing her mother, best friend, and collaborator devastated Faith. But she found comfort in her art, and she knew that Willi would want her to keep working. Remembering her family's history of storytelling, Faith added a new dimension to her painted quilts. Besides the visual images, Faith began to write stories to go along with the pictures on the quilts.

Church Picnic (from 1988) is one of Faith's many story quilts. The quilt shows a group of well-dressed people attending a picnic in a park. Along the top and the bottom of the image, Faith wrote the stories of the different characters she had created.

Faith also used her own life experiences to make the story quilts. The quilt *Tar Beach* is based on Faith's childhood. On hot summer nights, Faith and her family would go up to the tar roof of their apartment building and look at the stars. The adults chatted and played cards, and the kids ate snacks and lay on a mattress, looking at the heavens. Faith used her imagination to make this rooftop scene even more interesting. On the quilt, she painted a girl flying over top of the Washington Bridge, which is seen in the background. When Faith was little herself, she used to imagine she could fly and go anywhere she wished. In the story quilt, she made her dream come true.

A twenty-five-year traveling retrospective (an exhibit that shows an artist's work from the beginning of her career to the present time) opened in 1990 to honor Faith's work. It toured thirteen museums across the United States. The same year, Faith began her most famous series of story quilts, *The French Collection*. The quilts tell the story of Willia Marie Simone, a brave young Black woman who travels to Paris and becomes an artist. To work on the series, Faith traveled to France.

Going from story quilts to writing storybooks was a natural step for Faith. She wrote and illustrated her first children's book *Tar Beach* in 1991. It won *The New York Times* Best Children's Book Award, the Caldecott Honor for best illustrated children's book, and the Coretta Scott King Award for best illustrated book by an African American. Since then, she has written ten more books for young people. Faith also wrote a book for adults, published in 1995, called *We Flew Over the Bridge*. It is her autobiography and tells the story of her life an as African American woman and as an artist.

Today, Faith divides her time between both coasts of the United States. She works in a studio in her ranch house in New Jersey and is a professor of art at the University of California in San Diego. Faith continues to invent unique kinds of art, and it's exciting to think about what wonderful paintings and books she will create next.

Through her work, Faith combines personal experiences with storytelling and politics to inspire people all over the world. By believing in herself, Faith accomplished her dreams. She believes that doing so is possible for everyone.

> You can see examples of Faith's art on her website (**www.faithringgold.com**). The site also lists the museums where you can see her work.

MARY PRATT

1935 -

SHADOWS AND LIGHT

A particular challenge some women face is finding a balance between family responsibilities and their careers. Sometimes they can become so busy caring for others that their own dreams get pushed aside. Mary Pratt faced these difficulties. Because of her family responsibilities, she had little time for art. She seized every moment she could find to paint and develop as an artist. In Mary's work, we can see that all time is precious, and no matter how normal a moment may seem, there is always beauty in what we see every day.

Mary Frances West was born on March 15, 1935, in Fredericton, New Brunswick, on Canada's east coast. Her mother, Katharine, ran the household and raised and disciplined Mary and her little sister, Barbara. Mary's father, William, was a very successful lawyer who later became a Supreme Court judge and the provincial attorney-general. He was a traditional man and demanded proper behavior from his daughters. He believed that living an orderly life was very important. But he also had an artistic side and loved to paint in his spare time.

The Wests lived in a lovely house on Waterloo Row, and the girls had almost everything they could possibly want. They always had lots of toys: The backyard had a life-size playhouse, a sandbox, a see-saw, and a swing. Their father took pride in the gardens, so in the warm months, the yard was beautiful and green.

Despite having so many possessions, Mary was not quite satisfied. She knew from an early age that she wasn't interested in material things that she could hold in her hand. What she valued most were the colors and shadows she saw all around her.

Mary had a visual memory and could recall the way objects and colors looked at different times of the day. She was fascinated by light, the way it played on objects and created shadows. When she was six years old, she remembers draping a red sweater over the back of a chair. Mary couldn't stop looking at the bright spots where the sunlight touched the sweater and the little shadows that appeared in the ripples in the fabric. When she got home from school the following afternoon, someone had put the sweater away. She was so disappointed that she would never again see the sweater as it appeared at that moment.

Mr. and Mrs. Pratt wanted their children to be happy, confident people and always encouraged the girls when they showed talent. Mary was good at drawing. If her teachers wanted a student to draw something on the board, they always chose Mary. Judge West, seeing his daughter's interest in art, enrolled her in weekend art classes.

> "I've never wanted to paint what I did not know — intimately and sensuously. The look of things, the feel of things — their ability to arouse me — had led me along the paths you see in my pictures."
> —Mary Pratt

Mary found them boring, because the instructors didn't always let her draw what she wanted to draw. Mary pursued art outside of classes by drawing pictures and painting at home. In grade seven, she won first prize at a local competition for children's art, and her drawing was exhibited in Paris, France.

Although her father was an amateur painter, Mary actually did her first painting with her mother. Photographs were black and white when Mary was little, so people used to add a bit of color to their photographs by hand. This was called tinting. Using a cotton swab and some translucent paint, Katharine and Mary added hints of color to their family pictures. From then on, Mary created her own paintings.

Mary thought a lot about becoming an artist when she grew up, but she was a practical person. She wasn't sure if painting was a useful career, or if she could even make money doing it. Sometimes she thought of becoming a missionary or a minister, but she felt that art was the only career that would make her happy. Judge West made it clear to his daughter that he wanted her to nurture her talent. He encouraged her to go to Mount Allison University, in Sackville, New Brunswick, to study fine art.

In 1953, Mary began her classes at Mount Allison. Many of the fine arts teachers were accomplished artists, such as Alex Colville, Ted Pulford, and Lawren P. Harris (son of Lawren S. Harris, a founding member of the Group of Seven). Mary learned basic drawing and painting techniques. She took courses on still life and figures, where she practiced painting everything from wine bottles to live models. Her instructors praised her work, and she flourished at the university, surrounded by art, discussion, and knowledge.

One day when Mary was at a grocery store buying food — to paint, not to eat — she met a fellow student named Christopher Pratt. He suggested that instead of buying fruit to paint, as she had planned, that she should buy a whole fish and paint it laying on brown butcher paper. Mary took his suggestion. Christopher was from Newfoundland and was studying to become a doctor at the time, but he soon switched to the fine arts program. Mary had never met anyone with whom she had so much in common, and soon Mary and Christopher became close friends.

After receiving her Certificate of Fine Arts in 1956, Mary took a year off from school and moved to Newfoundland to be with Christopher. In September of 1957, they got married and embarked on an adventure to Glasgow, Scotland, where they both planned to study at the Glasgow School of Art. Soon after arriving in Europe, Mary found out she was pregnant and had to put her plans on hold. They spent about two years in Scotland, during which time Mary cared for their new son, John, and took care of the home. She was so busy with her new responsibilities that she had little time to paint at all.

The Pratts came back to Canada and both continued their degrees at Mount Allison. Mary was a fourth-year student, so she was mostly allowed to make her own schedule. Balancing her home life and her art was tricky, so the flexible hours were helpful, especially after Mary had her second child, Anne. In 1961, Mary's hard work paid off and she graduated with a Bachelor of Fine Arts.

Getting a degree while raising a family was a big accomplishment for Mary, but her life wasn't exactly as she'd hoped.

Because the children and the home were her responsibilities, painting often took a backseat to parenting. Christopher, meanwhile, devoted most of his time to his art and was becoming quite successful. The National Gallery of Canada bought one of his paintings, and he became the director of the Art Gallery at Memorial University. Mary struggled between feeling proud of him and feeling jealous because his dreams

Mary studied fine art and met her husband, Christopher Pratt, here at Mount Allison University in Sackville, New Brunswick.

were taking off while hers had been put on hold. When she asked an artist friend for advice, he told her that she should accept that in her family, there was only room for one artist — Christopher.

Things changed when Christopher became ill. He resigned from the gallery and the Pratt family moved to the small fishing community of Salmonier, Newfoundland. Mary felt strongly that she didn't want to live there. She felt isolated from the rest of the world. By this time, she also had four small, excitable children, all under the age of six (Barby and Ned were the youngest). Plus, she had to attend to her sick husband and give him emotional support when he doubted himself as an artist.

Mary felt her dreams of becoming a painter slowly moving out of reach. Her days were consumed by housework and children and schedules. She couldn't find the time to paint, but decided to make the time. Whenever she could steal a few precious moments, she picked up a brush and worked.

In 1967, Mary had sixty paintings exhibited at the Art Gallery of Memorial University. Her style was close to the impressionist style (where objects in a painting aren't shown exactly as they appear in real life). In the beginning, her subjects were things she saw every day, such as a bed or a fireplace. But Mary's style would soon change to become almost as realistic as a photograph.

On an ordinary evening in 1969, something inside Mary clicked. The Pratts had just finished eating dinner. The sun sat very low on the horizon, spreading a glowing orange light across the supper table. The plates, glasses, and leftover food cast long shadows. Mary was about to start her routine of

Mary's husband, Christopher Pratt, in 1976 with two of his paintings

clearing the table, but she stopped. She told Christopher and the children to go to another room, because she absolutely had to paint the scene.

Christopher replied that the light would disappear before she could even pick up a paintbrush, so he took a picture of the table. He made a slide from the negative and gave it to Mary. In the tiny bit of celluloid, Mary could see the shadows and light she had seen that night, and set about creating a beautiful painting from an ordinary moment.

Mary believed that painting *Supper Table* changed her artistically. Before, she'd always felt like she was preparing for something: preparing the kids for school, preparing dinner, preparing to get out her supplies to paint. But seeing the special light that would soon disappear made her realize that life was not about preparing. It was about action. She knew she had to go for it if she was ever going to make it as an artist. She had to start living her dream. To give herself more time to work, Mary hired a woman named Donna to help with the household chores. Donna also worked as a model and posed for some of Christopher's paintings.

With her creativity in full force, Mary painted for many hours a day. She often worked from photographs or slides to capture the light and shadows of her subjects. For example, in *Baked Apples on Tinfoil*, she worked for many days to get the reflection from the foil just right, and you can almost feel the warmth of the apples that have just come from the oven. She also painted pictures of chickens in butcher paper and herring that looked almost like photographs.

In the early 1970s, Mary's career took off. She exhibited work at the Morrison Gallery

> "A visual artist is born with a desire to find what is right, what is perfectly pleasing to the eye and brain and sense of textures — design, rhythm… to find a personal calligraphy."
>
> —Mary Pratt

in Saint John, New Brunswick, and had a show at Douglas Duncan's Picture Loan Society in Toronto. Some reviewers called her work "workmanlike and unsentimental," but many recognized Mary's unique ability to find beauty and light in objects that we might not notice. Mary also took to painting outdoors and drew on her childhood as inspiration. In *Waterloo Row, Fredericton*, from 1972, she painted the house and street where she grew up.

Painting subjects that showed domestic life drew Mary into the feminist movement. She never intended her work to be political, but her work and her story inspired many feminists. She became a role model for many women who felt they could not achieve their dreams because they were burdened with traditional work in the home. In 1975, Mary was invited to participate in an exhibition at the National Gallery of Canada called *Some Canadian Women Artists*. Showing at this gallery introduced Mary to a national audience, and her work was praised by critics as the "most memorable" of the exhibition.

But as Mary's success grew, so did the tension in her marriage. Christopher was an internationally respected artist who supported his wife, but their lives changed in big ways when both of their careers developed. There may have been some jealousy, and the Pratts probably found it difficult to focus on their relationship when their work and their children required so much attention. They stayed married despite the difficulties, but threw themselves into work and their children. They built separate art studios on their property where they spent a lot of their time working.

Confidence in her work allowed Mary to experiment with different subjects, and her work became more political at times. Some of the paintings she exhibited at the Aggregation Gallery in Toronto show this. *Service Station* shows a butchered moose carcass hanging in a garage. At first, she didn't want to paint it, but the image planted itself in her mind. By painting such a violent, forceful image, Mary said she wanted to make a "female statement about a male world."

Another new subject in Mary's work was the female figure. She painted Donna, her former housekeeper, from photographs that Christopher had taken. *Girl in a Wicker Chair* from 1978 and *Girl in My Dressing Gown* from 1981 were well received for their beauty and energy.

In 1981, the London Regional Gallery held a retrospective of Mary's work. Instead of feeling accomplished, Mary was slightly disappointed. She felt that her art hadn't developed as much as she wanted it to, and decided that it was time to seriously think about the direction she wanted her art to take. Although her style continued to be realistic, Mary became much more interested in the deeper meaning behind her images. "The reality comes first, and the symbol comes after. That's the way my work is," Mary decided. Inspired by the marriages of her two daughters, Mary's 1986 painting *Wedding Dress* shows a white dress hanging from a small tree. Some viewers appreciate the painting for how it looks, and others view it as a symbol of purity. The painting was also reproduced on the cover of *Friend of My Youth*, a book by the famous Canadian author Alice Munro.

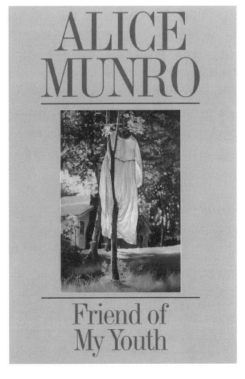

Wedding Dress on the cover of Alice Munro's book *Friend of My Youth*

By the 1990s, Mary Pratt had become a major figure of the Canadian art scene. In 1995, her paintings were included in two important exhibitions that toured across the country: *The Art of Mary Pratt: The Substance of Light,* her solo exhibition at the Beaverbrook Art Gallery in Fredericton, and *Survivors in Search of a Voice: The Art of Courage,* a group exhibition at the Royal Ontario Museum in Toronto.

Mary has received many awards and honors throughout her career. She has honorary doctorates from eight Canadian universities, she won the Canada Council of the Arts Commemorative Medal in 1993, and she was made a Companion of the Order of Canada in 1997.

Because she is always interested in learning, Mary has tried her hand at different art forms as well. Between 1994 and 2002, she worked on a series of woodcut prints with the famous Vancouver printer Masato Arikushi. In 2000, she came out with a book called *Mary Pratt: A Personal Calligraphy*, a collection of her personal writing throughout her career. Mary and Christopher are still married, but they no longer live together. They are still good friends, though, and see each other often to discuss their family and their art.

As the years go by, Mary finds that art becomes even more important to her than ever. She has come a long way as an artist. On the path from being a young mother who could barely find the time to pick up a brush to becoming a renowned painter, Mary's confidence and artistic talent have flourished. A true artist, Mary shows viewers the beauty in everyday objects, and how the most fleeting of moments are often the loveliest. She continues to paint and to become a better artist, striving to capture that perfect light.

You can see some reproductions of Mary Pratt's art by visiting the website of the Art Gallery of Newfoundland and Labrador at **www.heritage.nf.ca/arts/agnl/mpratt.html**

Resources

ARTEMISIA GENTILESCHI

Bal, Mieke (editor). *The Artemisia Files: Artemisia Gentileschi for Feminists and Other Thinking People.* Chicago: University of Chicago Press, 2005.

Danto, Arthur C. "Artemisia and the Elders." *The Nation.* April 8, 2002, p. 33.

Garrard, Mary D. *Artemisia Gentileschi.* Princeton, New Jersey: Princeton University Press,1989.

O'Neill, Mary. "Artemisia's Moment." *Smithsonian.* May, 2002, p. 52.

Wilkin, Karen. "Father and Daughter at the Met." *New Criterion.* April, 2002, p. 46.

ELISABETH LOUISE VIGÉE LE BRUN

Baillio, Joseph. *Elisabeth Louise Vigée Le Brun: 1755–1842.* Fort Worth: Kimbell Art Museum. 1982.

Evans, Sian (translator). *The Memoirs of Elisabeth Vigée-Le Brun.* London: Camden Press. 1989.

May, Gita. *Elisabeth Vigée Le Brun: The Odyssey of an Artist in an Age of Revolution.* New Haven: Yale University Press. 2005.

Sheriff, Mary D. *The Exceptional Woman: Elisabeth Vigée-Lebrun and the Cultural Politics of Art*. Chicago: University of Chicago Press. 1996.

EMILY CARR
Bogart, Jo Ellen. *Emily Carr: At the Edge of the World*. Toronto: Tundra Books. 2003.

Carr, Emily. *Klee Wyck*. Toronto: Irving Publishing. 1965.

Debon, Nicolas. *Four Pictures by Emily Carr*. Toronto: Groundwood Books. 2003.

Endicott, Marion. *Emily Carr: The Story of an Artist*. Toronto: Women's Educational Press. 1981.

Klerks, Cat. *Emily Carr: The Incredible Life and Adventures of a West Coast Artist*. Canmore: Altitude Publishing. 2003.

Newlands, Anne. *Emily Carr: An Introduction to Her Life and Art*. Willowdale, ON: Firefly Books. 1996.

GEORGIA O'KEEFFE
Berry, Michael. *Georgia O'Keeffe: Painter*. New York: Chelsea House Publishers. 1988.

Kucharczyk, Emily Rose. *Georgia O'Keeffe: Desert Painter*. San Diego: Blackbirch Press. 2002.

Mattern, Joanne. *Georgia O'Keeffe*. Edina, MN: ABDO Publishing Company. 2005.

Thomson, Ruth. *Georgia O'Keeffe*. Danbury, CT: Franklin Watts. 2003.

Turner, Robyn Montana. *Georgia O'Keeffe*. Toronto: Little, Brown and Company. 1991.

RESOURCES

FAITH RINGGOLD

Ringgold, Faith; Freeman, Linda; and Roucher, Nancy. *Talking to Faith Ringgold.* New York: Crown Publishers. 1995.

Ringgold, Faith. *We Flew Over the Bridge: The Memoirs of Faith Ringgold.* Toronto: Little, Brown and Company. 1995.

Turner, Robyn Montana. *Faith Ringgold.* Toronto: Little, Brown and Company. 1993.

Faith Ringgold's Website: www.faithringgold.com

LOUISE NEVELSON

Bober, Natalie S. *Breaking Tradition: The Story of Louise Nevelson.* New York: Athenuem. 1984.

Cain, Michael. *Louise Nevelson, Sculptor: American Women of Achievement.* New York: Chelsea House Publishers. 1989.

Glimcher, Arnold B. *Louise Nevelson.* New York: Praeger Publishers. 1972.

Lisle, Laurie. *Louise Nevelson: A Passionate Life.* New York: Summit Books. 1990.

Martin, Elizabeth and Meyer, Vivien. *Female Gazes: Seventy-Five Women Artists.* Toronto: Sumach Press. 1997.

Streifer Rubinstein, Charlotte. *American Women Sculptors: A History of Working in Three Dimensions.* Boston: G.K. Hall and Co. 1990.

FRIDA KAHLO

Laidlaw, Jill A. *Frida Kahlo.* Toronto: Franklin Watts. 2003.

Frazier, Nancy. *Frida Kahlo: Mysterious Painter.* Woodbridge, CT: Blackbirch Press. 1992.

Kent, Deborah. *Frida Kahlo: An Artist Celebrates Life.* Chanhassen, MN: The Child's World. 2004.

Woronoff, Kristen. *Frida Kahlo: Mexican Painter.* New York: Thomson Gale. 2002.

ELIZABETH CATLETT
Fax, Elton C. *Seventeen Black Artists.* New York: Dodd, Mead and Company, 1971.

Herzog, Melanie Anne. *Elizabeth Catlett: An American Artist in Mexico.* Seattle: University of Washington Press, 2005.

Lewis, Samella. *African American Art and Artists.* Berkeley: University of California Press, 2003.

Norment, Lynn. "Elizabeth Catlett: Legendary Artist Is Still Creating and Living Life on Her Own Terms." *Ebony.* March, 2006.

Sims, Lowery Stokes. "Elizabeth Catlett: A Life in Art and Politics." *American Visions.* April-May, 1998.

Streifer Rubinstein, Charlotte. *American Women Sculptors: A History of Women Working in Three Dimensions.* Boston: G.K. Hall and Co, 1990.

KENOJUAK ASHEVAK
Blodgett, Jean. *Kenojuak.* Toronto: Firefly Books. 1985.

Finley, Carol. *Art of the North: Inuit Sculpture, Drawing, and Printmaking.* Minneapolis: Lerner Publications Company. 1998.

Houston, James. "Northern Light: Kenojuak Ashevak." *Time Canada*. Dec 1, 2003, v162 i22 p.73.

Jimenez, Maria. "Art Is My Job: And My Job." *Globe and Mail*. Toronto. October 20, 2003, p.R1.

Leroux, Odette; Jackson, Marion E.; and Freeman, Minnie Aodla. (editors) *Inuit Women Artists*. Vancouver: Douglas and McIntyre. 1994.

Walk, Ansgar. *Kenojuak: The Life Story of an Inuit Artist*. Manotick, Ontario: Penumbra Press. 1999.

Library and Archives Canada: Celebrating Women's Achievements — Kenojuak Ashevak
www.collectionscanada.ca/women/002026-502-e.html

Dorset Fine Arts
www.dorsetfinearts.com/artist_kenojuak.html

"Eskimo Artist: Kenojuak."*Artists at Work*. National Film Board of Canada. 1987.

MARY PRATT

Lind, Jane. *Mary and Christopher Pratt*. Vancouver: Douglas & McIntyre. 1989.

Pratt, Mary. *A Personal Calligraphy*. Fredericton: Goose Lane Editions. 2000.

Smart, Thomas. *The Art of Mary Pratt: The Substance of Light*. Fredericton: Goose Lane Editions. 1995.

Life and Times: Christopher and Mary Pratt. CBC. 1997. (video)

Library and Archives Canada, Celebrating Women's Achievements: Mary Pratt
www.collectionscanada.ca/women/002026-519-e.html

Photo Credits

ARTEMISIA GENTILESCHI
All photos public domain courtesy Wikimedia Commons

ELISABETH LOUISE VIGÉE LEBRUN
All photos public domain courtesy Wikimedia Commons

EMILY CARR
Page 23: *Toronto Star* Archives
Page 28: *Toronto Star* Archives
Page 32: Emily Carr Institute, photo courtesy of Emily Carr Institute, photographer: Cari Bird
Page 33: Courtesy Jesse Hickman / www.jessehickman.com

GEORGIA O'KEEFFE
Page 35: Georgia O'Keeffe, ca. 1920. Image originally photographed by Alfred Stieglitz and is courtesy of the Miscellaneous Photograph collection in the Archives of American Art, Smithsonian Institution.
Page 39: Public domain courtesy Wikimedia Commons
Page 40: Alfred Stieglitz photographing Georgia O'Keeffe at Lake George, 1924. Image originally photographed by Arnold H. Rönnebeck and is courtesy of the Arnold Rönnebeck and Louise Emerson Rönnebeck papers, 1901-2000, in the Archives of American Art, Smithsonian Institution.
Page 42: Library of Congress, Prints & Photographs Division, Carl Van Vechten collection (LC-USZ62-42493)
Page 43: Library of Congress, Prints & Photographs Division, Carl Van Vechten collection (LC-USZ62-116606)

LOUISE NEVELSON
Page 47: © John Reeves
Page 50: Louise Nevelson as a young woman, ca. 1922. Image is courtesy of the Louise Nevelson papers, [ca. 1922]-1979, in the Archives of American Art., Smithsonian Institution.

Page 55: Louise Nevelson standing in front of her artwork at Pocantico Hills (Nelson Rockefeller's estate)], 1969. Image originally photographed by Impact Photos Inc., and is courtesy of the Louise Nevelson papers, [ca. 1922]-1979, in the Archives of American Art, Smithsonian Institution.

Page 57: Louise Nevelson with artwork in her studio, ca. 1974. Image originally photographed by Ara Guler and is courtesy of the Louise Nevelson papers, [ca. 1922]-1979, in the Archives of American Art, Smithsonian Institution.

FRIDA KAHLO

Page 59: Photo by Nickolas Muray, © Nickolas Muray Photo Archives

Page 62: Library of Congress, Prints & Photographs Division, Carl Van Vechten collection (LC-USZ62-42516)

Page 64: Frida Kahlo and Diego Rivera, ca. 1933. Image is courtesy of Albert Kahn papers, 1888-1973, in the Archives of American Art, Smithsonian Institution.

Page 65: Library of Congress, Prints & Photographs Division, Carl Van Vechten collection (LC-USZ62-103971)

Page 67: Frida Kahlo with *Self Portrait as a Tehuana*, ca. 1943. Image is courtesy of the Florence Arquin papers, 1923-1985, in the Archives of American Art, Smithsonian Institution.

Page 68: Frida Kahlo in her studio with *The Two Fridas*, Coyoacán, Mexico, ca. 1943. Image is courtesy of the Florence Arquin papers, 1923-1985, in the Archives of American Art, Smithsonian Institution.

ELIZABETH CATLETT

Page 71/76: © Fern H. Logan

KENOJUAK ASHEVAK

Page 81: © John Reeves

Page 86: Judith Eglington / Library and Archives Canada / PA-140297

Page 89-90: © Ansgar Walk

FAITH RINGGOLD

Page 93: Faith Ringgold © 2007

MARY PRATT

Page 103: © John Reeves

Page 108: *Toronto Star* Archives

Page 111: From *Friend of My Youth* by Alice Munro © 1990. Published by McClelland & Stewart Ltd. Used with permission of the publisher.

More from The Women's Hall of Fame series

978-1-897187-15-9

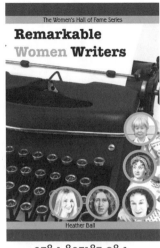

978-1-897187-08-1

978-1-897187-02-9

978-1-896764-98-6

978-1-896764-66-5

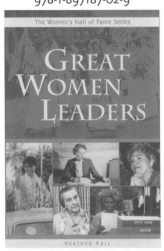

978-1-896764-81-8

978-1-896764-88-7

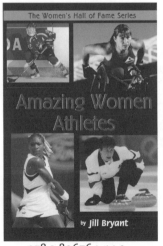

978-1-896764-44-3

978-1-896764-43-6

ages 9-13   • $10.95   •   www.secondstorypress.ca